READ
PEOPLE

RITA CARTER

READ PEOPLE

UNDERSTAND BEHAVIOUR.
EXPERTLY COMMUNICATE.

 WHITE LION
PUBLISHING

HIGH LIFE
HIGHLAND

3800 18 0079889 8	
Askews & Holts	16-Jan-2019
150	£12.99

First published in 2018 by White Lion Publishing
an imprint of The Quarto Group
The Old Brewery, 6 Blundell Street
London N7 9BH
United Kingdom

www.QuartoKnows.com

A catalogue record for this book is available from the British Library.

ISBN 978 1 78131 731 0
Ebook ISBN 978 1 78131 778 5

10 9 8 7 6 5 4 3 2
2022 2021 2020 2019 2018

Designed and illustrated by Stuart Tolley of Transmission Design

Printed in China

MIX
Paper from
responsible sources
FSC® C016973

CONTENTS

INTRODUCTION   08

HOW TO USE THIS BOOK   10

01 FACE TO FACE

01	First Impressions	18
02	How Dimensions Tell a Story	22
03	All in the Eyes	28
04	Signals	32
→	Toolkit 01—04	36
+	Further Learning	38

02 EMOTIONS AND EXPRESSIONS

05	Big Expressions	44
06	Small Expressions Tell the Most	48
07	Body Language	54
08	Displaying Yourself	58
→	Toolkit 05—08	62
+	Further Learning	64

03 PERSONALITIES AND HUMAN NATURE

09	Finding the Shape of Human Nature	70
10	Types and Stereotypes	74
11	How Personality Forms	80
12	Reading Others' Minds	84
→	Toolkit 09—12	88
+	Further Learning	90

04 COMMUNICATION AND INFLUENCE

13	Conversation Flow	96
14	Instinct v Influence	100
15	Confidence	106
16	Movers and Shakers	110
→	Toolkit 13—16	114
+	Further Learning	116

05 READING SOCIETY

17	Groups	122
18	Families	126
19	Groupthink	132
20	Crowds	136
→	Toolkit 17—20	140
+	Further Learning	142
	Epilogue	144

INTRODUCTION

Reading a person is a bit like reading a book that occasionally breaks into a foreign language. Most of the time we have (or think we have) a fairly good idea of what is going on when we interact with another person. What someone says is what they mean, and what they say they will do is what they do. Then, for some apparently inexplicable reason, they do something else. Such behaviour is perplexing, irritating and frequently hurtful.

Some of these rifts in communication occur because someone deliberately wants to deceive. More often, they happen because the person doesn't know what they think or why they are doing something. This is when it is useful to know that other language – the one that is conveyed through the body, by facial expressions and, sometimes, via seemingly irrational behaviour.

Read People is an introduction to that language. It translates the physical signs that tell of a person's life experiences and analyzes their facial expressions, gestures and body language to expose their true feelings and intentions. It also reveals some of the psychological and biological mechanisms that drive people to behave in curious and complicated ways.

Most of these mechanisms are unconscious. In fact, most of what we do and think is unconscious. Most of us know from personal experience that we can do something quite complicated – driving a car home or humming a familiar song – without consciously attending to it. Recent studies of the unconscious show that it is also capable of forming sophisticated and long-term plans and carrying them out without the person consciously knowing they even have a plan. In one study, participants were primed (informed of something without them realizing it) to cooperate before starting a lengthy and complex interactive game. They subsequently pursued a strategy similar to another group of people who were consciously trying to cooperate. By contrast, a group that had neither been primed nor told to cooperate were competitive throughout.

The assumptions we make about people because they happen to fall into some particular slot in our mental filing system affect how we behave far more than we know.

Similarly, the unconscious assumptions we make about people because they happen to fall into some particular slot in our mental filing system affect how we behave far more than we know. The ability to distinguish friend from foe helped early humans survive, and we make up our mind about people before we even know we have seen them. Looking at why and how this happens, we can learn to use this innate skill without abusing it. These lessons become even more crucial to understand when people come together into a group or crowd, especially in extreme situations when hive or mob psychology becomes dominant.

Read People is not meant to be a full explanation of human behaviour (an impossible endeavour), but provides a series of tools to help you find explanations for yourself. Reading people must always be approached with care, but as the speed and forms of communication in our world become ever faster, these tools are more important than ever.

HOW TO USE THIS BOOK

This book is organised into five parts and 20 key lessons covering the most current and topical debates within behavioural psychology today.

Each lesson introduces you to an important concept,

and explains how you can apply what you've learnt to everyday life.

As you go through the book, TOOLKITS help you keep track of what you've learnt so far.

At BUILD+BECOME we believe in building knowledge that helps you navigate your world. So, dip in, take it step by step or digest it all in one go – however you choose to read this book, enjoy and get thinking.

Specially curated FURTHER LEARNING notes give you a nudge in the right direction for those things that most captured your imagination.

YOU ALREAD
THE ABILITY
FACES; IT'S
RIGHT INTO
BRAIN.

Y HAVE
TO READ
BUILT
YOUR

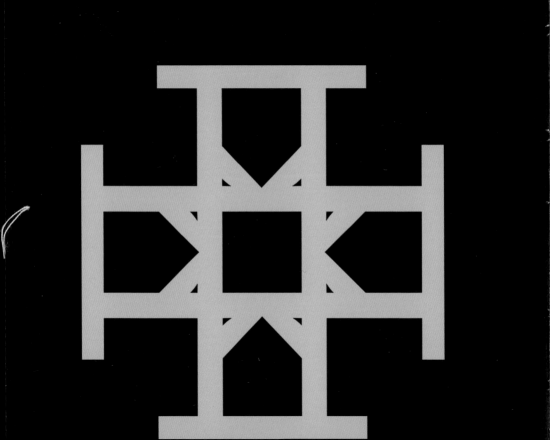

FACE TO FACE

LESSONS

01 **FIRST IMPRESSIONS**
What you can tell about someone in one tenth of a second.

02 **HOW DIMENSIONS TELL A STORY**
The face shape associated with domination and dishonesty.

03 **ALL IN THE EYES**
If you look closely into those eyes, you are looking at a brain.

04 **SIGNALS**
How your life is written on your face.

We are compelled to scrutinize the faces of people who might affect us for information about what they are thinking and feeling.

The human face is the most fascinating object in the world to other humans. It tells us things about its owner as loudly, and sometimes more honestly, than speech or action. We are therefore compelled to scrutinize the faces of people who might affect us for information about what they are thinking and feeling.

Knowing these things about others is of vital importance to us because we live in such a deeply interconnected society. Many of our actions are constrained by others, and 'reading' their faces allows us to adapt our own actions in order to manipulate them, please or appease them.

The loudest signals that come from a person's face are conveyed in expressions – voluntary or unconscious movements of the facial muscles. These, combined with speech, are so powerful that they often drown out the more subtle messages that can be seen in the structure of the face itself. We recognize many of the signals intuitively, but often fail to take note of them.

In the first chapter of this book we look at the human face in the way that a paleontologist might examine a fossil – deducing behaviour from its physical form rather than from what it does. This section looks at four important lessons.

If you can read a face carefully, by the time a person deliberately starts communicating – through expression, speech or gesture – you will already have some idea of their history, personality traits and likely behaviour.

FIRST IMPRESSIONS

You already have the ability to read faces; it's built right into your brain. The skill is so important that we have evolved a brain system dedicated to face-reading and it works with astonishing speed. Before we are even conscious of seeing a person, an ancient, hard-wired cognitive system makes a complex judgement about them based on the shape, form, proportions and expressions of their face. It decides first whether the person is attractive or repellent, and then whether they are competent, trustworthy, extrovert or dominant.

Do you know that feeling of distrust or recoil when you meet a stranger, even one who is behaving impeccably? If you don't, it's probably because you override your seemingly inexplicable intuitions about people, preferring to concentrate on more rational ways of judging them.

Instant reaction
(unconscious):
One tenth of a second
Conscious reaction:
0.5–10 seconds

Burning cheek of embarrassment

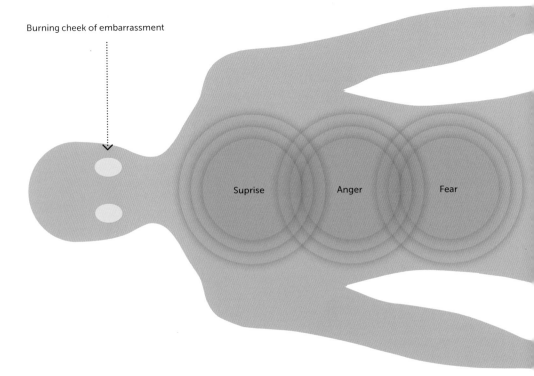

Suprise

Anger

Fear

Gut reactions seem to come from nowhere and be based on nothing. They can't be assessed or double-checked, and they happen as a result of calculations that are not accessible to us – processes we may not even know are happening. It seems irrational to take any notice of them.

In fact, there is a very good reason to note them. The ability to make instant, largely unconscious judgements about faces has proved so useful to us that evolution has written it into our genes. It is our primary strategy for distinguishing between friend and foe but, like most of our built-in defences, it is pretty crude. Yet, intuitive face-reading has stuck in our genes because – on the whole – it works.

Confronted with an unfamiliar face, you will make quite a complex judgement about its owner within one tenth of a second. Your brain will judge whether the person is trustworthy, attractive, likeable, competent, aggressive or peaceable. All of this happens before you know consciously that you have seen them! When the face stays in view long enough to make a conscious judgement (from half a second to 10 seconds), your initial judgement is unlikely to change significantly. The only big difference is that you get more confident about it. First impressions are not only fast – they last. We refer to 'gut reactions' because our digestive tract is massively endowed with nervous tissue which reacts intensely to emotional events. Emotions are also felt throughout the body: think of the 'burning cheeks' of embarrassment, the 'weak knees' of foreboding, or the trembling hand of anxiety. Even gut reactions are different according to the emotion experienced: fear is frequently felt quite low in the abdomen, while anger is felt higher up, in the stomach or above.

Trembling hand of anxiety

Weak knees of foreboding

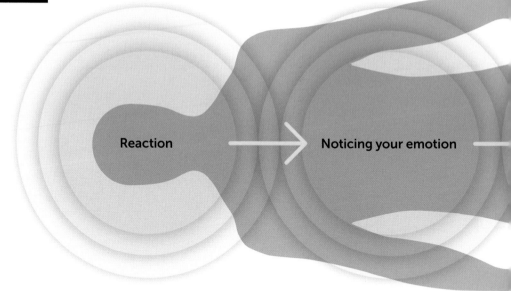

Reaction → Noticing your emotion →

SNAP JUDGEMENTS

For many of us, making snap judgements feels wrong. Our initial feeling about a person tends to be fleeting and easily drowned out by the subsequent onslaught of information we receive as we interact with them. We may not notice a tiny flutter of fear or attraction or, if we do, we may dismiss it as meaningless. This is a mistake, but it is one that is frequently made by many of us.

Indeed, the judgements we make instantly are very likely to be the same as those made by people who know the person well.

You don't have to know how the face-reading brain trick works to make it work for you. When you meet someone new, you can enhance your natural face-reading skills by attending to your own feelings and behaviour, as well as to those of the other person.

First, get familiar with your emotions. Start by noting when you have an emotion that you experience physically – butterflies or a spontaneous frown, for instance. Emotional thoughts are just side-shoots of emotion, the core of them is an alteration in body state.

Next, identify the emotion and put a name to it. Don't limit yourself to the obvious ones like joy, anger, fear and so on; recognize the hybrids too – the mixture of fear and elation you get before a fairground ride, or the combined sadness and sweetness of nostalgia. Once you have identified what emotion you are feeling, take time to examine exactly what physical effect it is having on you.

Although emotions produce typical physical reactions, we are all slightly different, so learn to identify your own responses. When I am fearful, I feel two small cold patches just below my cheekbones. A friend of mine says she feels fear in her upper arms.

Identifying the emotion ⟶ **What is the physical effect?**

Now scrutinize your biases. Some people are very sensitive to threat, while others are exceedingly trusting. And life events – abuse at the hands of a person with a particular type of face, say – can alter one's reactions to such a face, even at an unconscious level.

So, while you should always take note of your reactions, you should also factor in these biases: if you know you habitually feel fear at the sight of a stranger, try overriding your intuition just a little.

In one study researchers asked volunteers to gauge the competence of a lecturer on the basis of a two-second clip of the teacher talking. Their quick-fire verdicts more or less matched the judgements of students who had been taught by the professors for an entire term. The same group have shown that the leadership ability of corporation bosses can be assessed surprisingly accurately by a glance at their photo. They asked volunteers to look at pictures of chief executives of the top 25 and the bottom 25 companies in the Fortune 1,000 list and judge how good they thought the person they were looking at would be at leading a company.

The results of their study showed that the students' assessments of the leadership potential of the bosses were significantly related to their company's profits. What's more, the instant judgements were more accurate than those of senior managers rating the bosses they actually worked for.

HOW DIMENSIONS TELL A STORY

You can tell certain things about a person just by looking at their face, even when they are not wearing any particular expression. Dominance, conscientiousness, sociability, intelligence and even criminality can be detected – more accurately than by chance – with just a mugshot to go on. We do some of this face-reading unconsciously, and recent scientific work has uncovered some of the physical giveaways that our brain picks up on – minute differences in the structure, form and proportion of the head and facial features.

The idea that a person's character is stamped on their face is an ancient one. The Greek philosophers even compiled a volume of the ways in which a person's face reflected their 'spirit'. 'Impudence', the treatise says, is evident in 'bright, wide-open eyes with heavy blood-shot lids'. A broad nose, meanwhile, is described as a sign of laziness.

There is not a shred of evidence to link impudence with bloodshot lids, or a broad nose with laziness, but fact and nonsense have always been inextricably mixed in the long and sometimes dubious history of physiognomy.

In recent years, a few scientists have re-examined the possibility that personality traits can be detected from physical clues. There is one personality revealing

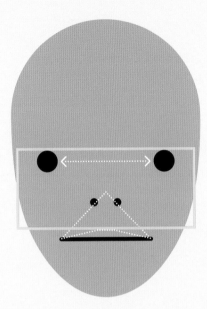

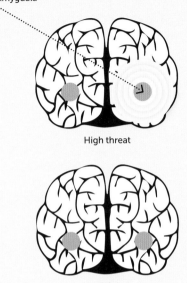

Amygdala

High threat

Low threat

facial characteristic that is both proven and well understood: people with bigger cheekbones and wider faces are on the whole more dominant, more aggressive and less honest than those with narrower-shaped faces.

The test for a high width-to-length ratio is simple: measure the width of the face across the highest point of the eyelids, then measure the length from this line to the top of the upper lip. A high ratio is anything over 1:9. You don't have to whip out a tape measure to do this when you meet someone though – this is one of the face structures that we recognize intuitively.

Wide faces are more common in men than in women because they develop largely due to the effect of testosterone, a hormone that is generally more prevalent and effective in males. From before birth and throughout maturity, testosterone moulds both the brain and the body. In the brain, it stimulates part of the amygdala – the brain's emotion generator – which produces an aggressive reaction to threat. It also damps down the connections between the amygdala and the 'thinking' areas of the brain, reducing the degree to which a person can control their drives, urges and emotions. In the face, testosterone promotes the growth of cheekbones and the jaw.

THE FACE OF LEADERSHIP – AND DECEIT

The correlation between wide faces and certain types of behaviour has been demonstrated dozens of times. In one study, men with various face widths were invited to pretend to be property salesmen trying to offload a piece of land which had a prohibition on future development. A group of pretend buyers were meanwhile instructed to purchase only land that could be developed. The sellers' honesty was then measured according to the extent to which they misled their buyers. Those with wide faces were found to be significantly more likely to tell lies to secure a sale.

Other studies have found similar evidence for antisocial behaviour in wide-faced males, but also some big advantages. Sportsmen with broad cheeks commit more fouls than others but also score more goals.

The situation with women's faces is more complicated than for men. Although wide female faces are perceived to indicate leadership qualities, recent research suggests that female faces with exactly the opposite structure – narrow and heart shaped – are also seen to indicate likely leaders. The researchers based their findings on a series of studies. These included one in which volunteers were asked to assign certain competition-themed statements, such as, 'She wants it her way or you're out', and, 'He treats others with respect to a degree, but mostly believes he is right', to images of men and women which had been digitally altered to accentuate or minimize facial gender characteristics. More than 50% of study participants associated statements such as, 'She was feared by those around her', or, 'There is only one boss, and that is her' with both a low-masculinity and high-masculinity image of the same woman. For male images, the statement, 'Co-workers consider him very driven', was associated by 64% of participants with high-masculinity images compared to 33% for low-masculinity images, while the statement, 'Doesn't tolerate people trying to act like they are smarter or wiser than he is', had a 63% link to a high-masculinity image compared to 27% for a low-masculinity image.

One of the researchers, Jochen Menges of Cambridge University, explains, 'Our study challenges gender theory that says women with feminine facial characteristics are associated with communal behaviour and nurturing – feminine-looking women have a better chance of being seen as leaders than previously thought.'

There's some evidence that we can overcome the personality signals given off by our static facial structure simply by pulling the right facial expressions – see Chapter Two, Lesson 5. Beware, then, of making judgements based on facial features alone, since we can easily be fooled. The science of physiognomy is still young, the research patchy and the findings complex. Facial structure has some validity as a way of reading people, but many factors – such as education, intelligence and parental influence – can cancel out the 'natural' personality traits signalled by the face. We should be very cautious of drawing conclusions about a person's character based on their looks, as history has repeatedly shown.

Men whose faces are wider than they are long are more likely to be ambitious and elected as leaders. Wide-faced political candidates are more likely to win elections than narrow-faced adversaries, and a high width-to-length face ratio increases the likelihood that its owner will negotiate better deals and earn more money.

COUNTLESS
HAVE SHOW
PEOPLE PRE
SYMMETRIC
FEATURES.

STUDIES

N THAT

ER

AL FACIAL

ALL IN THE EYES

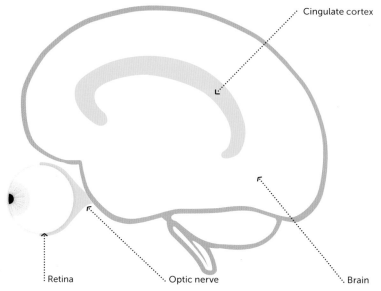

Cingulate cortex

Retina

Optic nerve

Brain

When you gaze into a person's eyes, you are looking at their brain. Their eyeballs are the outer part of two projections of nervous tissue that form a pathway that ends at the back of the head. Put like that, it doesn't sound very romantic, but it explains why our own eyes are drawn so strongly to the eyes of others, and why eye-to-eye contact can feel so overpowering. When we see a change in someone's eyes we are seeing an alteration in their brain – no cover up is possible.

We may not be aware of it but, when we look into someone's eyes we are scrutinizing them for minute changes – primarily in pupil size and gaze direction – along with the effect of the facial muscles around the eyes. These are some of the most powerful signals people give, and we will be looking at them in detail in the next chapter.

This lesson, however, looks at a less well-known phenomenon – the link between behaviour and eye colour, eye structure and other static eye characteristics.

Eye formation is driven in part by genes, which also fashion the anatomy of other parts of the brain. One example is the Pax6 gene, which (among other things) helps develop tissue in the iris and in a part of brain called the cingulate cortex. This is an important bit of our brain because it acts as a sort of buffer between the deep limbic portion – where our emotions are generated – and the frontal cortex – where we process those emotions and work out a rational response. Depending on how the cingulate cortex has developed, it primes us either to favour grabbing and pursuing the things we encounter in the environment

Fuchs' crypts

(approach-related behaviours) or to hide or flee from them.

Dense tissue in the left-side cingulate will promote approach-oriented behaviour – that is, the person will be inclined to reach out to others, to empathize with them, and to trust and generally like them. Thin tissue development in that area inhibits approach-oriented behaviour and encourages an impulsive 'fight or flight' reaction.

Pax6 mutations have a similar effect on tissue development in the iris. Low tissue density in the iris is indicated by little squiggly lines that radiate out from the pupil known as 'Fuchs' crypts'. A team of researchers led by Mats Larsson at Örebro University in Sweden studied 428 subjects and found that people with more crypts (plus other signs of low tissue density) were less likely than others to be warm, outgoing and trusting and were more neurotic. The Swedish researchers counted the crypts of their volunteers using elaborate laboratory equipment but you can do a much rougher analysis just by looking at someone's eyes – high-density irises are smooth and homogenous, while those with many crypts have a much greater variation of shade and pattern.

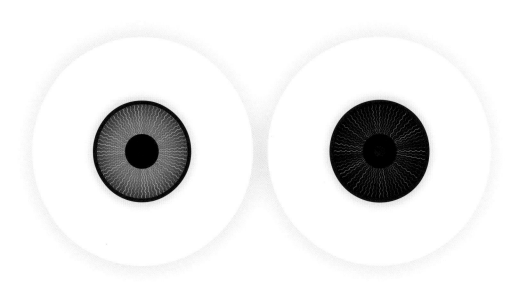

EYE COLOUR

Similar eye-gene-brain links are thought to account for various correlations between eye colour and behaviour. Eyes are darkened by melanin and the genes that promote it are also at work in the brain, helping to build the insulation sheaths that allow electrical messages to pass from one neuron to another. Good insulation means swift and accurate information processing, with minimum loss of signal. This may account for a whole raft of correlations between dark eyes and personality.

Brown or hazel eyes Researchers at the University of Pittsburgh found that people with brown or hazel eyes felt more pain during childbirth and were more likely to suffer postpartum depression or anxiety than women with blue eyes.

Dark eyes Other studies have found that dark-eyed people are more susceptible to alcohol, and thus — because they don't need much of it to feel the effect — are less likely to become alcoholics.

Dark-eyed people react faster, and there is some evidence to suggest that they think faster than light-eyed people too, though not in such depth.

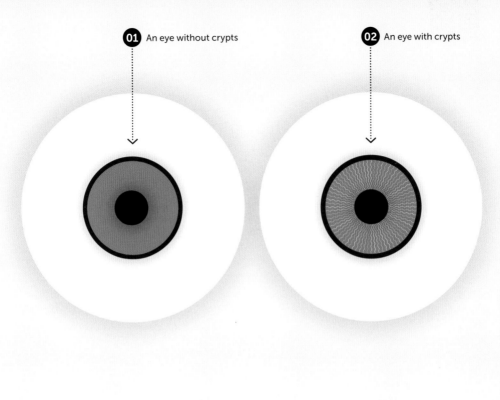

01 An eye without crypts   **02** An eye with crypts

A study of people's perception of eye colour and behaviour found that people with dark eyes are thought to be more dominant than those with light eyes.

Although there is evidence and rationale to back up eye-behaviour links, it is still important to be cautious about them. A huge number of factors determine human personality – most of them still unknown.

Genetic inheritance is undoubtedly one factor, but the environment can distort or even completely reverse an individual's 'natural' personality. Even before birth, our environment has influenced our development – identical twins will be ever so slightly different at birth just because one has been in one part of the mother's uterus and the other in another part.

01. **An eye without crypts. This sort of smooth, homogenous iris is associated with people who are drawn to others.**

02. **Crypts show up as squiggly lines and dark patches radiating from the pupil. This densely crypted form of iris is associated with people who are less trusting and more impulsive.**

SIGNALS

As well as revealing certain inherent personality traits, a person's face conveys many things about their lifestyle, health and behaviour. The signals are subtle, and to read them you need to look beyond the deliberate messages conveyed by expressions, and ignore for the moment the cosmetics, hairstyle, spectacles and other 'add-ons' a person may wear. You need to look instead for the marks – some temporary and some indelible – that a person's life has left on their face.

Countless studies have shown that people prefer symmetrical facial features; this is particularly true where sexual selection is concerned. The most popular explanation is that symmetrical features indicate 'good genes' – suggesting that a person with such features is good mate material.

Another explanation is that facial asymmetry arises from illness or injury during gestation or in childhood.

Researchers at Edinburgh University examined the facial features of 292 people aged 83 and compared their facial symmetry with detailed information about their social status during childhood, including their parents' occupations and how crowded their home was.

The researchers studied 15 different 'landmarks' on the face, including the positions of the eyes, nose, mouth and ears, and found a strong association between upbringing and the symmetry of the face. Those with more symmetrical faces had more privileged and easier upbringings than those with asymmetrical features. The effect was stronger in men than women, and interestingly, events in later life had no effect on facial symmetry. Even those who went on to have healthy and wealthy lives continued to carry the mark of childhood deprivation.

Those with more symmetrical faces had more privileged and easier upbringings than those with asymmetrical features.

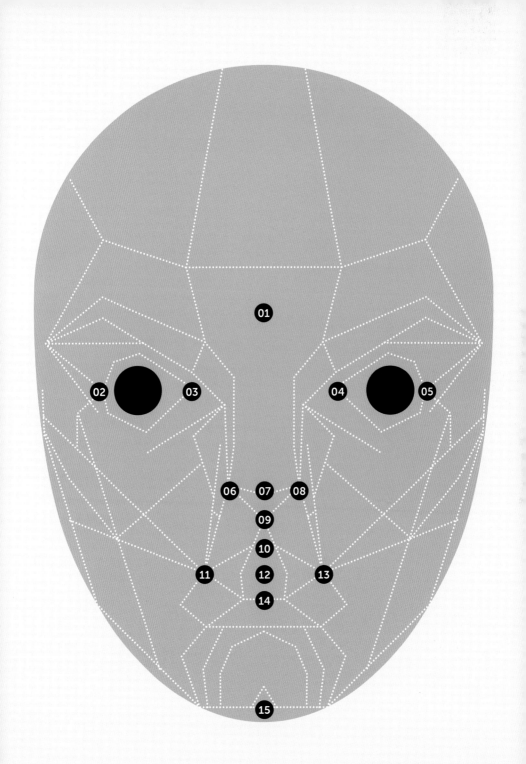

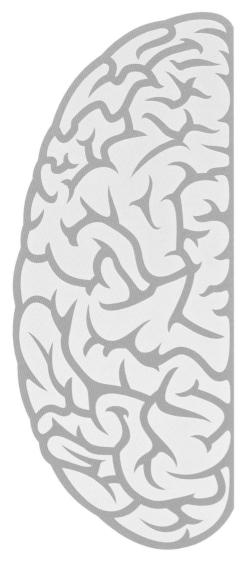

SIGNS TO LOOK FOR

Each brain hemisphere controls movement on the opposite side of the body, so the muscles around the left side of the mouth are controlled by the right hemisphere and vice versa. The hemispheres generate different types of behaviour. In most people these differences are very slight because the brain hemispheres work so closely together that the messages they send to the body are 'as one'.

Fearful, shrinking behaviour is generated by the right hemisphere and determined action comes from the left hemisphere. These personality traits are displayed on the face by differing muscle movements:

01. Social A 'social' smile will be slightly more prominent on the right side, for instance.

02. Internally conflicted People who are internally conflicted may show greater differences between their left and right sides. Someone who naturally tends towards right hemisphere-style behaviour but constantly has to play the extrovert is likely to have a more lopsided smile than a person who is whole-heartedly outgoing. Over time, these differences produce visible changes in the landscape of the face due to unequal activation of the facial muscles on each side. As people get older, these asymmetries become more marked. People with symmetrical faces have been found to be more outgoing and agreeable, while those with asymmetrical faces are more neurotic.

03. Age A person's age is written very obviously on their face, but the way a face ages says as much about a person as the inevitable wrinkles. In 2015, researchers at the Chinese Academy of Sciences used computer imagery to generate 3D models of over 300 people's faces (aged 17 to 77). They used these models to look for correlations between specific facial features and age. They found, for example, that, older people tended to have wider noses and more sloping eyes. Some people had faces that were 'young' for their age based on these markers, with any two people of the same chronological age differing by around six 'face years' on average.

Facial age correlated more strongly with objective markers of health, such as cholesterol levels, than with chronological age – showing that a person's lifestyle is indeed written on their face.

Here is one way to reveal small asymmetries in a person's face. Take a photo of them front on and, using a computer drawing programme, divide it vertically, make mirror images of the two halves and join the mirror images to the originals to make two entirely symmetrical faces.

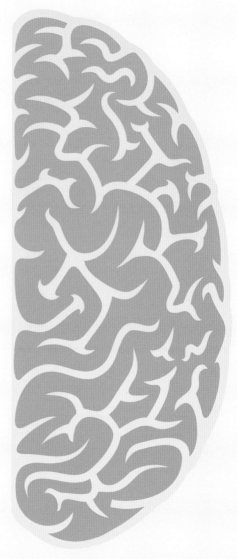

TOOLKIT

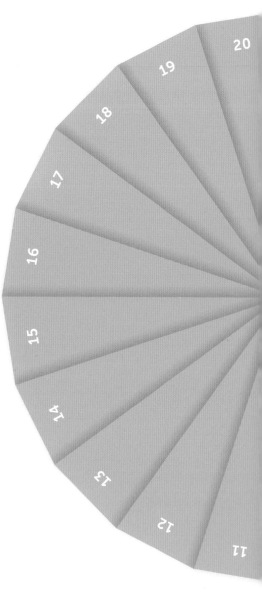

01

We assess a person on the basis of their face even before we know we have seen them! This unconscious assessment produces a 'gut reaction' that is often right. You can tune into this useful signal by attending to your own feelings when you first meet someone.

02

Bone structure shows the effect of sex hormones in development. Wide cheekbones and a large jaw are associated with stereotypically masculine characteristics, such as dominance and assertiveness.

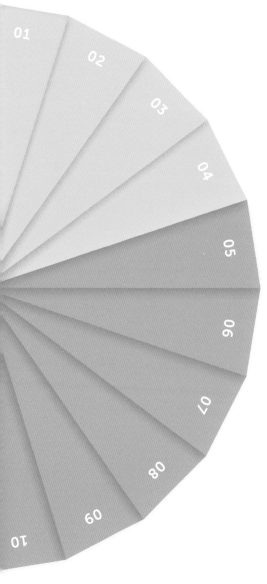

03

Eyes are an extension of the brain and the clearest indicator of what is going on in someone's head. Emotional changes produce corresponding alterations in pupil size, while iris colour and formation can indicate particular personality traits.

04

Facial symmetry gives a clue to a person's background and personality. Lopsided features suggest a deprived childhood and may indicate psychological conflict. Although these facial markers have been scientifically validated, they can easily be overwritten by environmental factors, so they should be treated with caution.

FURTHER LEARNING

READ

Face Value: The Irresistible Influence of First Impressions
Alexander Todorov
(Princeton University Press, 2017)

The Human Face
Brian Bates with John Cleese
(DK Publishing, July 2001)

First Impressions: What You Don't Know About How Others See You
Ann Demarais and Valerie White
(Bantam Books, 2005)

About Faces: Physiognomy in Nineteenth-Century Britian
Sharrona Pearl
(Harvard University Press, 2010)

WATCH

The Human Face
BBC films

The Hidden Power of Smiling
Ron Gutman
TED Talk

VISIT

National Portrait Gallery
St Martin's Place, London, WC2H 0HE

EMOTIONS AND EXPRESSIONS

LESSONS

05 BIG EXPRESSIONS
Facial expressions are part of emotion, but they can be faked.

06 SMALL EXPRESSIONS TELL THE MOST
What lies beneath the smile?

07 BODY LANGUAGE
How emotions affect the whole body.

08 DISPLAYING YOURSELF
The messages people wear.

Signals that are made consciously may also be deceptive – there is often good reason for a person to put out misleading information about themselves.

Human communication is a two-way street; just as you need to read other people in order to know how they will treat you, they need to signal their characteristics, intentions, mood and personality to you.

Much of this signalling is deliberate. Visually obvious messages, such as big smiles, frowns, expansive gestures and obvious displays of dress, are intended to convey information to those watching. The messages may be quite honest; that is, the message they convey is genuine. The smile means a person is pleased to see you, while the smart dress reflects a person who is careful and sharp in character. But signals that are made consciously may also be deceptive – there is often good reason for a person to put out misleading information about themselves.

In this chapter we will take a look at the visual signals that convey what people are like, what they feel and how they relate to us. We'll show how to distinguish between deliberate signals, which may be misleading, and unconscious 'tells' that cannot be faked.

BIG EXPRESSIONS

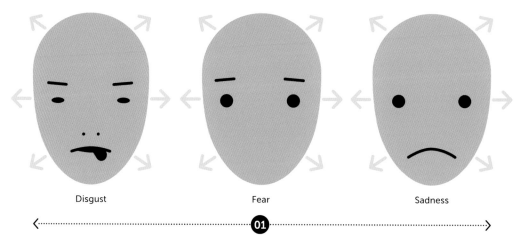

Disgust   Fear   Sadness

01

Charles Darwin first suggested that facial expressions are 'built in' and are therefore similar in every culture. The idea has since been supported by hundreds of scientific studies. Although facial expressions may be modified by culture – ideas of politeness for instance – the difference is slight. They are as natural to us as wagging a tail is to a dog.

There are six universal expressions that signal the same thing in every human culture and society. They are outward signs of the basic emotions of fear, happiness, disgust, anger, sadness and surprise.

These expressions are the same (or very similar) in everyone because they are part of the emotion itself. Unless you actively inhibit your facial movement, you will automatically screw up your nose and eyes if you, say, step on a piece of dog excrement, and you will inevitably raise your eyebrows and open your mouth if you are suddenly surprised.

To understand why expressions are universal, it helps to grasp one surprising fact about emotions: they are not essentially feelings. Emotions are bodily changes. These physical changes have evolved to steer us towards things that can help us survive, and away from things that could harm us.

01. Disgust, fear and sadness all drive us away from the things that trigger them.

02. Joy and anger propel us towards the things that trigger them.

03. Surprise is a 'freeze' reaction, designed to keep us still until we get more information.

For example, if your brain senses a threat or a challenge – perhaps by registering a rustle in the bushes – it raises your blood pressure and heartbeat, reduces peripheral blood flow and primes certain muscles for movement.

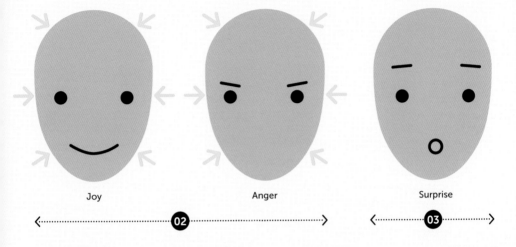

Joy

Anger

Surprise

02

03

These changes prepare the body to fight or flee. They comprise the core emotion of fear, not any subsequent feeling.

If you forget that expressions are 'signs' and think of them instead as physical adaptations, they become easier to understand. For example, an expression of disgust involves closing your mouth tight and narrowing your nostrils by wrinkling your nose. This helps to prevent any noxious matter from getting inside your body. Surprise will make you raise your eyebrows and open your mouth. These movements increase the input of sensory information – your eyes open up and your mouth can take in any airborne taste or smell molecules.

You might expect facial expression to begin *after* the 'feeling' – a sort of 'icing on the cake' of emotion. This is not so – facial contortion is one of the bodily changes that comprises the emotion, and therefore happens right at the start of an emotional reaction.

The reaction starts before we are *able* to register the stimulus. Think of the saying 'catch a smile'. Faced with a smiling face, we start to smile back – even before we are conscious of seeing the face that bears the smile.

The feeling of fear only occurs if the deep-seated, unconscious brain areas that generate emotion send strong enough messages to the conscious cortex. When this happens, the person will usually 'feel' their fear. In some people, this happens easily while in others it takes a far greater stimulus to activate cortical areas. Nervous, cautious people are likely to be in the first category, while those who enjoy dangerous sports and function well on a battlefield are likely to be in the second.

FAKING OUR SIGNALS

'Big' expressions can be brought under conscious control and faked or suppressed. Learning to tell the difference between one facial expression and another, and to tell when an expression is 'genuine' or at odds with a person's inner feelings are very useful skills to develop.

Once emotions are 'felt', our conscious mind modulates them, either amplifying ('Ahh, it's a tiger – I'm going to die!') or dampening them down ('No worries – it's only the wind rustling'). Consciously changing some parts of the emotion – heart rate, for instance – can be quite difficult, but facial muscles are easy to control. Our brains register our expressions and react as though they are genuine. So, we can fool ourselves as well as others.

Convincing fakery is difficult, however, because most expressions include the movements of muscles that are not under conscious control. Method actors overcome the fakery problem by trying to produce the essential emotion rather than just faking the external sign of it.

Let's look at the smile as an example. Smiles are produced by contracting the muscles that pull your lips back and up. In addition, spontaneous smiles cause contractions of the little muscles around the eyes. The cheek muscles are easily contracted consciously, but the eye muscles are more difficult to manipulate – about 30% of people are unable to contract them at will. 'Social' or 'fake' smiles can therefore often be spotted by the extent to which the eye muscles are contracted.

To distinguish a fake smile from a real one, concentrate on the eyes. The tiny muscles around them are difficult to control and usually contract only if a person genuinely feels pleasure or warmth. Look out for a narrowing and elongation of the eyes, and the appearance of a little bulge underneath them.

As well as signalling emotion, facial expressions can amplify or even create an emotional reaction. In one experiment, people were asked to hold a pencil in their mouth and try writing with it. One group held the pencil horizontally in their teeth, which forced them to smile, while another group held it between their lips, which forced them to frown.

The volunteers were told they were part of an experiment to help people with limb disabilities, but the activity was really designed to find out if the facial expressions the volunteers were forced to adopt affected their emotional state. It seems they did. When the volunteers were asked to say how much they enjoyed a set of funny images, the ones who had been forced to smile found them significantly funnier.

SMALL EXPRESSIONS TELL THE MOST

As well as making the obvious 'macro' expressions, people produce tiny, momentary facial changes that they can't easily control and probably don't even know about. These 'micro' and 'subtle' expressions occur when people are trying not to show what they are thinking or feeling. The feeling may show for a split second in the twitch of a nostril or a very slight puckering of the brow. It is easy to miss these fleeting giveaways, but when you know what to look for, you can learn to spot and decode them.

When a person experiences an emotion and has no reason to conceal it, they typically show it on their face for somewhere between half a second and four seconds. Micro expressions are ghostly shadows of these 'macro' expressions. They flash across the face in an instant, lingering for half a second or so, but sometimes coming and going so quickly that they are impossible to spot in real time. Subtle expressions on the other hand may be quite long-lived, but they are very faint and easy to miss.

In 1966, psychologists Ernest Haggard and Kenneth Isaacs set out to see if people gave non-verbal clues about their feelings during consultations with therapists. They made video recordings of psychotherapy sessions then watched them in slow motion, scrutinizing every frame for tiny facial expressions. They found that these expressions occurred when the patients were trying either to hide their feelings from themselves (known as repression), or deliberately trying to conceal their feelings from the therapist (known as suppression).

This sparked interest in further analysis of fleeting expressions. In one famous series of experiments, psychologist John Gottman filmed married couples talking about their relationships, then studied their faces frame by frame, noting the slightest expressions. Using this almost imperceptible data, Gottman predicted with 90% accuracy which of the couples would get divorced, and when.

Around the same time, psychologist Paul Ekman studied a number of patients who had been diagnosed as seriously depressed, but who hid their condition. In the very first case, when the films were examined in slow motion, Ekman and his colleague Wallace Friesen plotted micro-facial expressions that revealed strong negative feelings the patient was trying to hide. Paul Ekman and his colleagues subsequently discovered subtle expressions. These last longer than micro movements but involve very slight, barely perceptible changes in facial muscles.

When a person displays a subtle version of a facial expression, it can either convey that the person has just begun to feel the emotion associated with that expression or that they are trying to hide their feeling. If the expression becomes more obvious it shows that the subtle expression was the dawning of the emotion, while if it fades it suggests the person is trying to conceal the feeling.

Macro

Micro

Subtle

Neutral

Subtle expressions are about 20% as intense as macro expressions

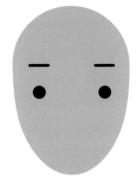

01. **Pleasant surprise** A quick up and down of the eyebrows.

HOW TO SPOT A LIE

Ekman has done more than anyone else to study every type of expression, and he has developed systems for identifying and scoring them for speed and intensity. He claims that almost anyone can learn to see these tiny signs. In particular, he has focused on the ability to recognize whether a person is lying.

The ability to spot when someone is deceiving you is obviously very useful, but it is not simple because there is no single expression – micro, subtle or macro – that indicates lying. Rather there are facial expressions that reveal that the speaker is stressed, anxious or uncomfortable – feelings that commonly occur when a person is trying to deceive. The important thing is to read these signs in the context of the situation, and particularly with regard to what the person is saying.

A good way to practise your new skill is to find an online video of an interview with a person who is likely to be anxious or known to be lying. News items with politicians are a good source. Turn off the sound and watch the person's face very closely, discounting the 'big' expressions and instead looking for faint or very fast muscular movements, especially around the mouth and eyes.

Repeat sections in which you think you can detect these signs until you can clearly discern them and know what you are seeing – is it a slight downturn of the mouth? A muscle twitch below the eye? Given that micro and subtle expressions differ from macro expressions only in duration and intensity, you should be able to work out what these tiny signs indicate. Now turn the sound back up and listen carefully to what the person is saying when the expressions occur. What was being said as the micro expression flashed? Did it match the words? If it didn't, there is a good chance that the person was not being entirely truthful.

02. Nasty surprise Eyes narrowed or squinting.

03. Contempt Lips turned up on one side only.

04. Anger/Aggression Lower jaw jutting forward, brows pulled together.

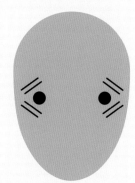

05. Fear Twitching of muscles around the eyes or cheeks.

06. Disgust Wrinkling around the nose, narrowed eyes and pulled-down brow.

07. Sorrow Raised eyebrows on either side of the nose; both lips downturned or pouting.

A DOMINANT
MAY HAVE M
EXPANSIVE
THAN A SHY
EVEN WHEN
FEELING DE

PERSON
ORE
GESTURES
INTROVERT,
THEY ARE
FEATED.

BODY LANGUAGE

Facial expressions give the most obvious signals about what a person is feeling, but the rest of their body transmits equally strong messages when you know how to read them. Body language is often more revealing than someone's face, because it is invariably unconscious.

Reading body language is challenging because to do it well involves considering many factors: the person's personality, what they are saying and the entire context of the encounter. Much of this information is normally unavailable, but you can nearly always discern a person's emotional state, and to some extent their personality, by noting how they move, stand and interact physically.

Like facial expressions, body language is universal. This is evident from several experiments using what is known as 'point light' displays. Typically, an actor will be kitted out with tiny lights on various parts of their body – shoulders, knees, hips, head, hands and so on – and will then parade in a darkened room so that only the pinprick lights are visible. In one such experiment, the actors were instructed to walk in the way that they might if they were sad, excited or scared. Observers from many different countries were invited to watch the moving lights, and

to identify from them the emotion that was being displayed. They got it right in nearly every case. Interestingly, fear was identified most accurately – probably because our brains are primed to recognize danger very quickly. This was followed by anger, disgust and sadness.

The experiment suggests that emotions affect the whole body and, like facial expressions, they are displayed in more or less the same way in every culture.

However, body language does differ from person to person because everyone has a different 'baseline' that dictates how clearly they display emotions. This baseline is determined by the extent to which a person inhibits emotion. This is largely a matter of extroversion and confidence – a dominant person may have more expansive gestures than a shy introvert, even when they are feeling defeated.

In some cultures, however, emotional displays are frowned upon and so even the most extroverted individual will learn early in life to inhibit gross displays of emotion. This of course adds a layer of difficulty to interpreting a single behaviour when it is someone you don't know, but looking at what makes up the baselines is still an insightful process.

Point-light displays allow people to see basic body language without distraction, as in this 'sad' walk.

READING THE BODY

Body language is universal, obvious and very influential, yet we often fail to note it consciously. That means we often fail to use it effectively, both to read other people and to influence them. Conscious awareness can be increased by noting each aspect of a person's body language and by analyzing it, rather as you might analyze a poem line by line in order to end up with a holistic understanding of it.

In one study that included videos of 2,000 business negotiations, one very simple thing made a difference – crossed legs. Not one negotiation ended in agreement when one party had their legs crossed. This fascinating study points to the power of body language – in this case showcasing resistance – over speech and facial expressions. Yet, despite it seeming obvious at times, it is one of the least consciously used forms of communication.

POSTURE

Confidence Erect posture and limb-spreading, especially combined with apparent relaxation, signals confidence, dominance and authority. Note how political leaders tend to throw their arms wide when addressing a crowd, or how a would-be leader often puts an arm around a rival in a show of apparent friendliness, but with the effect of reducing their stature.

Lack of confidence Anxiety, fear and lack of confidence tend to produce slouching shoulders and a tight and constrained posture.

Resistance Crossed arms and legs signal resistance to your ideas.

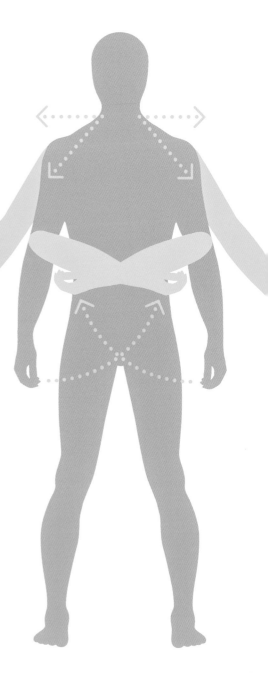

MOVEMENT

Anxiety Individuals who are anxious tend to fidget and fiddle with their hands. Sometimes they tap their feet or have jittery legs.

Shyness Looking down at the floor suggests shyness, timidity or embarrassment.

Fearfulness Fearful movement is jerky and hesitant, and people tend to turn sideways-on to others, shifting their vulnerable torso away.

Cheerfulness People who feel cheerful and secure move easily and energetically, walking with long, sweeping strides and allowing their arms to swing.

Sadness Sad movements are most obvious in the upper torso – a slight slump in the shoulders and a bowed head.

Impatience Exaggerated nodding signals anxiety about approval or possibly impatience. You need to see it in context.

Aggression Pointing at people usually signifies aggression or arrogance, while pointing a finger in the air suggests certainty and authority.

Confidence Large, expansive gestures suggest confidence.

MANIPULATING YOUR MOVEMENTS

> Extending your arms with palms turned down creates a sense of calm and forcefulness, or can show you are rigid and want control.

> Stretching out the arms with palms turned up is an invitation to agreement. When done with a jerk of the shoulders, it can mean resignation.

> Clenched fists usually connote resolve or anger. Conversely, they may show you are nervous and trying to 'harden up'.

> Rubbing hands together indicates stress. A 'hand-washing' gesture may signify anticipation.

> Steepling – arranging your hands with just the fingertips touching – displays thought, careful listening or self-assurance. It also suggests power.

INTERACTION

> Copying another person's movements shows that you are in tune with them, and may be a sign of affection or attraction.

> Physical closeness and touch also signal liking.

> Foot position is a powerful signal: if a person's feet point towards someone else, it suggests they are interested in them; whereas if one or both feet point away, it may mean they are bored or would like to be gone.

> Dominant individuals tend to lead the way, literally – entering rooms first and walking in front of others. An exception is where a person tries to exhibit high status by ushering another in front of them – a form of patronizing.

DISPLAYING YOURSELF

How we dress – from the clothes we wear to the way we style our hair and decorate our bodies – is a deliberate indicator of our personality, self-image and at times, even our world view. In every sense of the word, we 'dress to impress' – to make a statement to the world about who we are and how we want the world to see us.

Both sexes use the way they dress to project an image of themselves that is often intended to subtly deceive. One study looked at how people dressed on dates. It found that men tended to dress in their most expensive or conservative clothes. Their choice seemed to be geared towards appearing to be more financially secure or more of the 'commitment' type. Women, by contrast, wore clothes that drew attention to what they thought were their best physical features.

People probably started to wear clothing for protection, but as far back as we can go in history, we see signs of it being used to reflect identity, alignment with a particular group, to show status or riches, or as a sexual invitation. Today, self-presentation through dress is universal – you can even buy books on it or take courses in how to use clothes to project a particular image. Wear red, you may be told, to project confidence and sexuality; grow a bit of stubble to look cool. Many dress styles have become formal codes: apart from the obligatory uniforms worn by, for example, police constables and soldiers, there are conventional 'uniforms', such as suits for business people and lycra body suits for athletes.

However, these conventions make it more, not less, difficult to interpret a person by their dress. After all, nobody's wardrobe is all red; some stubbly men have simply forgotten to shave; bankers also jog and off-duty soldiers go to supermarkets. In other words, to understand what someone's dress is saying about them, you need to take into account the whole person and the context in which you see them.

When a person comes to a job interview in a smart suit, for instance, it doesn't tell you that they are diligent and business-like, but it does tell you they want the job and are smart enough to wear appropriate clothes for the occasion. If, by contrast, a person turns up to a formal event in torn jeans, it might mean they are disdainful of formality and generally rebellious, or it might mean they just made an embarrassing error. You would have to observe their demeanour (embarrassed? apologetic? defiant?) to know.

Another complicating factor is that people are affected by the clothes they wear. One experiment showed, for example, that when people put on a white coat they believed belonged to a doctor they became more mentally agile, and women who did a maths test in a swimming costume performed worse than a matched group who were dressed normally. Hence, to a small extent, if a person dresses smart, they *are* smart.

DRESS CODES

There is a great deal of consensus about what certain clothes indicate and, as these notions are well publicized, it is easy to use them for effect or even for manipulation.

For example, the commonly accepted idea that women who wear red are sexually available and more friendly than others is thought to account for the fact that waitresses who wear a red T-shirt receive up to 26% more in tips than those wearing other colours.

Dressing in a particular way has also been found to alter the way that people think. In one experiment, volunteers were asked either to dress in their normal clothes, or their most formal ones. They were then given a list of actions and asked to choose between abstract and concrete descriptions for them. For example, 'voting' could have a broad, rather abstract meaning such as 'influencing the election', or a more concrete interpretation, such as 'marking a ballot'. Those wearing formal dress favoured the more abstract meaning.

In another experiment, 54 college students were asked to bring two sets of clothing – one formal and one casual – to a study ostensibly about how people form impressions based on clothing. They were randomly assigned to change into one or the other of the sets of clothing, and then given a test that measured whether they were more focused on the big picture or on more fine-grained details. The test involved looking at a series of large letters made up of smaller letters, and then saying quickly which letter they saw. Those dressed formally were more likely than others to select the big letters, suggesting they were more focused on the 'big picture'.

Although much is known about the way people interpret others' dress, very little research has been done into the validity of those interpretations.

Curiously, one of the most telling dress items seems to be shoes. In one experiment, researchers assessed the personalities of a group of people, then gave descriptions of their shoes to another group who had never met them. They found that the second group judged the personalities of the shoe-owners much better than by chance.

Some of the findings were that people who wear high-top shoes tend to be less agreeable than those who show their feet, and that anxious people tend to wear dull shoes. Certain assumptions proved wrong though: participants assumed that people who wear more attractive and well-kept shoes tend to be more conscientious, but this did not turn out to be true.

AAAAAA
AAAAAA
A A
A A
AAAAAA
AAAAAA
A A
A A
AAAAAA
AAAAAA

HHHHHH
HHHHHH
HH
HH
HHHHHH
HHHHHH
HH
HH
HHHHHH
HHHHHH

EE
EEEE
EE EE
EE EE
EE EE
EE EE
EEEEEE
EEEEEE
EE EE
EE EE

SS SS
SS SS
SS SS
SS SS
SS S SS
SS S SS
SS SS
SS SS
SS SS
SS SS

TOOLKIT

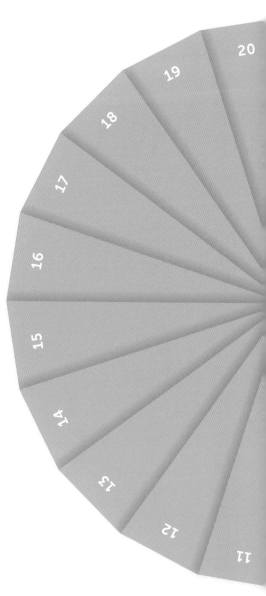

05

The way people present themselves
– through facial expressions, body
language and dress – may be conscious or
unconscious. Conscious presentation may
be deceptive, so look for the unconscious
signals as well as the obvious. If someone's
deliberate presentation is congruent with
their unconscious messages, the person is
probably showing their 'genuine' self.

06

Facial expressions are part of the emotion
that is being felt, not just a sign of it.
Even when 'big' expressions are inhibited
or faked, people invariably show fleeting or
subtle expressions that genuinely reflect their
feelings.

07

Body language is usually genuine and reflects, faintly, what a person wants to do physically. Their feet will point towards where they want to go, for example, and they will move towards things, or people, that they like.

08

The way a person dresses conveys the loudest signals about them – but also the most tricky to read. Everybody dresses differently for different occasions, so it is unwise to judge a person by their dress on a single meeting. Remember that people dress to impress, and the image they project may not truly represent who they are.

FURTHER LEARNING

READ

Emotions Revealed:
Understanding Faces and Feeling
Paul Ekman
(Orion, 2003)

The Definitive Book of Body Language: How
to Read Others' Attitudes by Their Gestures
Allan Pease and Barbara Pease
(Orion, 2017)

The Presentation of Self in Everyday Life
Erving Goffman (Penguin, 1990)

Body Language for Dummies
Elizabeth Kuhnke
(John Wiley & Sons, 2015)

WATCH

Lie to Me
Drama series starring Tim Roth

Can you really tell if a kid is lying?
Kang Lee
TED Talk

How to Spot a Liar
Pamela Meyer
TED Talk

STUDY

Paul Ekman International
Offers a range of online courses covering
facial expressions.
www.ekmaninternational.com

VISIT

Fashion museums
Historic fashion collections are an insightful
way to examine how clothes have historically
been used to signal status.

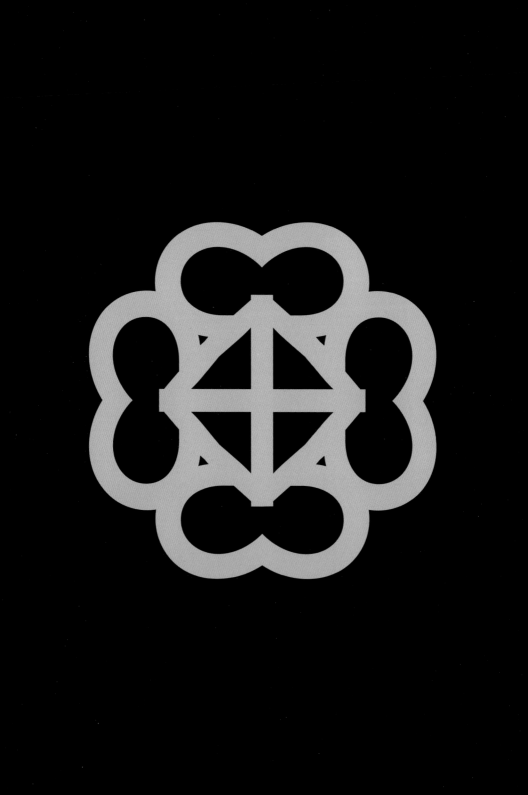

PERSONALITIES AND HUMAN NATURE

LESSONS

09 FINDING THE SHAPE OF HUMAN NATURE
Everyone has a unique personality and each one fits in to a particular pattern.

10 TYPES AND STEREOTYPES
How to put round pegs into round holes.

11 HOW PERSONALITY FORMS
What makes you 'you' and her 'her'.

12 READING OTHERS' MINDS
The skill that makes society stick.

We can only know the tiniest handful of people personally, yet almost every interaction with another person calls out for us to know something about them.

There are more than six billion people in the world and every one of them is unique. We can only know the tiniest handful of people personally, yet almost every interaction with another person calls out for us to know something about them.

In casual encounters, we usually have to take the other person's characteristics on trust. For example, when we ride on a bus, we make split-second judgements on where to sit, as we want to be confident that the person we sit next to will not be violent or rude.

But what about the bus driver? Merely hoping that they are competent and sober is not enough – we want to be sure. Most of the time we can be, because people entrusted with responsible jobs are almost certain to have been tested for basic competency and for having a suitable personality.

Measuring, charting and describing human personality is called psychometrics. In recent years it has become a precise science, and also the foundation of a vast industry. Practically every one of us is subjected to psychometric analysis either directly – if we apply for a job with a big corporation, for example – or indirectly, by the (usually hidden) scrutiny that is made of the information we give about ourselves when we buy something, visit a website or fill in a feedback form.

Psychometrics has developed tools that make it possible to know a great deal about an individual on the basis of small bits of information. In the following four lessons, we integrate these 'bits', piecing them together to decipher how we can expertly read each other.

FINDING THE SHAPE OF HUMAN NATURE

Sir Francis Galton was an excessively energetic 19th-century character who – between inventing forensic fingerprinting, exploring the tropics, promoting eugenics and devising the first weather map – found time to go through an entire dictionary looking for words that indicated personality.

Galton outlined 1,000 words and sorted them into groups that he thought were related – for example, talkative, outgoing and gregarious went into one group, while fearful, anxious and cautious went into another. In around 1936, this method was taken up by psychologists Gordon Allport and Henry Odbert, who scoured Webster's New International Dictionary, arriving at some 18,000 relevant words. They too tried to categorize them, but ended up with a huge and incoherent data set. It needed someone to sort it out into a usable tool.

That someone turned out to be the eccentric psychologist Raymond Cattell, who determined to use the information to uncover the largely hidden 'shape' of human personality. During the 1940s, Cattell persuaded thousands of people to rate themselves and others on the 18,000 words. Then he worked out which behaviours most frequently occurred together in an individual and which were completely independent. For example, he found that a person who is anxious is much more likely to get depressed

too. Knowing that someone is anxious, however, gives no clue as to whether they are caring, trusting or open to new ideas.

Cattell used his ratings to compile groups of words, like Galton's, which contained all the words related to each other but none that were independent. After many years of analysis, he announced that there were 16 such groups, and by rating an individual accurately on each of them you could describe any personality fully.

For the later part of his career, Galton was aided by the use of one of the first big computers, the ILLIAC I – a machine built by Illinois University, where he later taught. As computing developed, other researchers were able to undertake even more complex analysis of personality data, and as a result, the 16 factors uncovered by Cattell were gradually boiled down to five personality dimensions: openness, conscientiousness, extroversion, agreeableness and neuroticism. Today these are known as the Big Five, the Five Factor Model or by their acronym, OCEAN.

Theoretically, each dimension is independent of the others, although the characteristics within each group are related in a precise mathematical way. So for instance, if a person is anxious, they are 75% more likely to be depressive than someone with a low anxiety rating, and if

Extrovert

Talkative
Bold (socially)
Energetic
Gregarious
Assertive
Thrill-seeking
Cheerful
Enthusiastic

Agreeable

Warm
Kind
Cooperative
Trusting
Friendly
Open
Forgiving
Team-worker

Conscientious

Organized
Efficient
Methodical
Dutiful
Tenacious
Dependable
Hard-working
Responsible

Stable

Even-tempered
Satisfied/content
Relaxed
Optimistic
Self-accepting
Tolerant
Laid-back
Self-sufficient

Open-minded

Creative
Questioning
Artistic interests
Emotionally open
Adventurous
Liberal
Romantic
Playful

they are gregarious, they are 22% more likely to enjoy travelling. These findings have been turned into a test comprising hundreds of statements on which a person is rated (or rates themselves) for agreement on a 1–5 scale. A typical statement would be, 'I make friends easily,' or, 'I vote for liberal candidates'.

There is a great deal of controversy about personality tests because of their obvious limitations, but it has not prevented psychometrics (as personality measuring is called) becoming a vast industry.

THE BIG FIVE

If you want to work for a big company, fly a plane or adopt a child, you will almost certainly be subjected to some form of personality assessment. A survey of companies with dedicated Human Resources departments found that 75% use psychometric testing for recruitment and most have faith in the test results to the extent that they use them at least partly to determine who they employ.

The Big Five test (with many truncated versions available) provides you with a broad-brush description of your personality that will give you a better guide to your strengths and abilities than you will get from simply thinking about them. This can enable you to question how your personality helps, and perhaps hinders, you in important areas of your life. You really need to do a Big Five questionnaire to clearly see which dimensions are strongest in you, but you can get some idea by looking at the descriptions in the circles on page 71 and noting which match your personality most closely.

descriptions in the circles on page 71

✛ PRACTICAL TIP

01. Are any of my traits getting in the way of what I want to do or be?
02. Is there a particular dimension rating that explains why I am good or bad at what I do? If so, what do I need to do to change it?
03. Do any of my traits create opportunities that I am currently not pursuing? If so, how can I better make use of these traits?

This type of thinking is a personal exercise that can help you to reflect and, perhaps subtly, change how you respond to others. For example, you may realize that the person you have been thinking of as aloof or cold is actually just low on extroversion and needs a little more space than others. The irritatingly fearful person may be high on neuroticism, and quite unable to help feeling negative emotions.

Knowing personality dimensions will not change them, but it will allow you to understand people a little better, perhaps seeing their 'flip' side.

If your score is low on conscientiousness, you will almost certainly be familiar with accusations of carelessness in your work. The Big Five tells you, though, that people who are like this are also very likely to be spontaneous and flexible, so you might want to seek a job where these qualities are highly valued. You may find it's better to be self-employed rather than part of a large company, for example.

If your score is high on openness, you may have been told you question things too much or get bored too easily. However, the Big Five tells you that these qualities tend to go with inventiveness, so rather than stay around people who dislike your questioning stance, you might do better in a place where your ability to overthrow convention in favour of new ways of doing things is welcomed.

First look at each of the words in the circles on p.71 and rate yourself or the person you are analyzing on a scale of 0–5 for each one. Add the scores in each column and divide by 8, then mark the resultant number on the relevant 'spoke' of the wheel. Join the marks to arrive at your personality 'shape'. For instance, a score of 4-5-2-1-3 would give you the shape below.

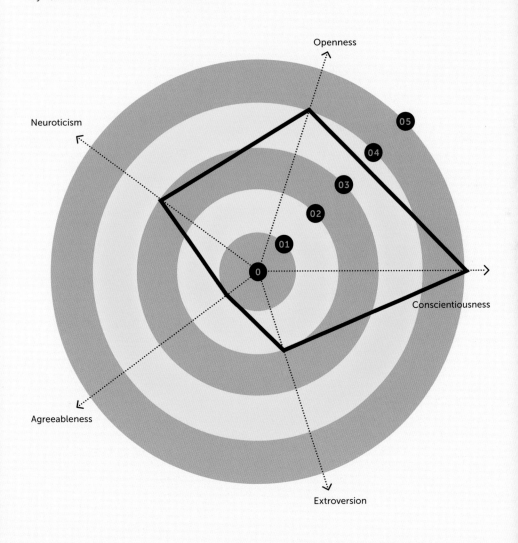

Openness

Neuroticism

05

04

03

02

01

0

Conscientiousness

Agreeableness

Extroversion

TYPES AND STEREOTYPES

The perfect personality test is one that would allow you to know everything about a person just by ascertaining one tiny piece of information about them. Astrology works like this – all you need to divulge is your birth time and in return you get a detailed character assessment. Unfortunately, astrology has no scientific basis, so it would be unwise to use it for anything but fun.

There are, however, typology systems that have proved groundbreaking and useful. By getting someone to complete a personality test you can, in theory, learn more about them than you would otherwise know through months of ordinary acquaintance. They use a similar process – extrapolating a great deal from a few facts – and have been validated by many studies. Of the many typologies that categorize personality, the best known is the Myers-Briggs Type Indicator (MBTI). It was developed in the 1930s and 1940s by two American autodidacts, Katharine Cook Briggs and her daughter, Isabel Briggs Myers. Their system borrows from Jungian psychology to arrive at 16 different types of personality, for which they developed a letter system – each of which is described by a combination of four letters.

There are also some systems which derive from different roots altogether. The Enneagram, for instance, claims to draw on Gurdjieff, Sufi philosophy and the Bible.

The Enneagram divides personalities into nine main types – Reformer, Helper, Achiever, Individualist, Investigator, Loyalist, Enthusiast, Challenger, Peacemaker – and then further divides them into subtypes: sexual, social and self-preserving. Sexual types instinctively look for and form close one-to-one relationships for security, social types draw support from groups and self-preservation types basically look out for themselves. If a crowd of people was suddenly subjected to a threat – an earthquake, say – the sexual types would grab their nearest and dearest and hang on, the social types would run with the herd, and the self-preservation types would react directly to the threat in whatever way seemed most likely to save their lives.

THE MYERS-BRIGGS TYPE INDICATOR
I (Introvert) or E (Extrovert); S (Sensing) or N (iNtuitive); T (Thinking) or F (Feeling); J (Judging) or P (Perceiving). So an ISTJ is an Introverted, Sensing, Thinking Judge, and an ENFP is an Extroverted, iNtuitive, Feeling Perceiver.

When you have completed the lengthy series of questions, you will be slotted cleanly into one of the types.

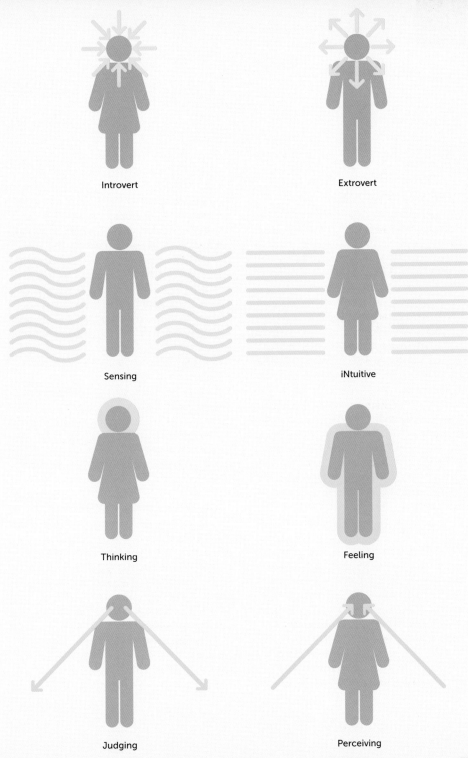

Introvert

Extrovert

Sensing

iNtuitive

Thinking

Feeling

Judging

Perceiving

TYPE BEHAVIOURS

Typology tests invariably comprise questions or lists of statements to which you must answer yes or no. Like the Big Five test, they basically require you to describe yourself and then return the description in an elaborated form. Though this sounds like a very basic method, it is surprisingly useful.

Let's say your test has identified you as an ESFP (Extrovert, Sensing, Feeling Perceiver) on the MBTI, or maybe a Type 7 (Enthusiast) on the Enneagram, and you have an issue you need to sort out with a colleague. From your point of view, you are a friendly person who likes to talk things over with people, and you feel that a spontaneous, direct, cheerful approach will be the most helpful. So you pop your head around your colleague's door and – as they don't appear to be doing anything – start talking about the issue.

To your irritation, your colleague does not seem pleased to see you and seems reluctant to talk about the issue. You fail to sort it out but when you return to your desk, you find an email from the colleague suggesting a meeting the next day to discuss it. As you had just been talking to them, their email, and the idea of a meeting, feels frustrating. From your point of view, the person has been unfriendly, unhelpful and generally rather unpleasant.

Now, imagine yourself in the shoes of the colleague – an INTJ on the MBTI, or an Enneagram Type 5 (Observer) – and let's see things from their point of view. You are mentally working through an issue when a colleague looks in, interrupting your thought process. They proceed to talk about the issue, stating their own views and leaving it to you to interpolate yours – which you prefer not to do as you have not yet worked them through. They jump about from one aspect to another, making jokes and deviations, and muddying what you had started to clarify in your own mind. The atmosphere chills, and by the time they go, you feel anxious and less clear about the problem than you were before. Recognizing that your colleague wants to sort the issue out urgently, you decide to act immediately by emailing them to suggest a meeting the next day – by which time you will have thought things through.

These types of interaction happen quite frequently, and although you don't have to be familiar with personality typology to know that people see things in different ways, it can help to be able to recognize types, especially those that are very different from you.

Typology tests can help you to see characteristics that you only hazily recognize in yourself (or in someone else), and help you to understand 'type' behaviours in others, leading on to being able to recognize patterns of behaviour more readily. Isabel Briggs Myers claimed of her test, 'When people differ, a knowledge of type lessens friction and eases strain. In addition, it reveals the value of differences.'

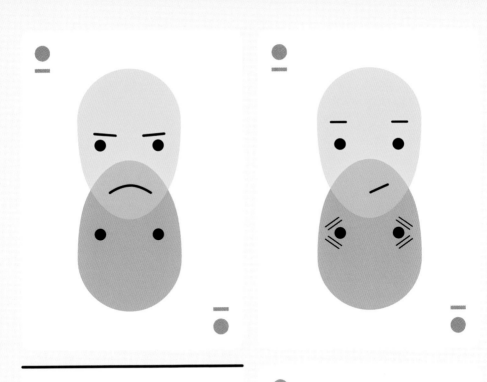

'Typing' people through a rigorous test is not the same as stereotyping – that is, assuming things about people because one of their characteristics is linked in your own mind to another.

As we've seen, certain characteristics are very often bundled together in individuals, but personality tests are designed to discern such linkages only when they really exist. One of the dangers of merely assuming that two characteristics are linked is that people 'live up' to the stereotype, perpetrating the error.

IT IS COMM
PEOPLE TO
SECOND PE
OR EVEN MU
'MINOR' ON

ON FOR
HAVE A
RSONALITY,
TIPLE
S...

HOW PERSONALITY FORMS

Ideas

Speech

Cultural trends

Mino

Have you ever seen someone you know acting really out of character? Perhaps you ran into a normally quiet, solitary colleague behaving outrageously at a party? More shocking still, someone tells you about a habit you weren't aware of.

Although most people have a major sustained personality, it is common for people to have a secondary personality, or even multiple 'minor' ones that pop up in particular circumstances. A few people display a kaleidoscope of behaviours that change with their roles and seem entirely unrelated to one another – conscientious worker, impatient parent, powerful lobbyist and appeasing spouse. Others may have a strong major personality but exhibit a behavioural quirk that is wholly at odds with their normal self. It may just be a strange gesture, an anachronistic phrase or an uncharacteristic habit, such as a finicky person dipping chocolate biscuits messily into their tea.

The number of 'minor' selves in a person varies greatly from individual to individual, but studies suggest that most people have at least four and some more than 20, with the average being around seven. Many of these are practically unnoticeable – fragments are picked up unknowingly from others, particularly in childhood when young minds suck up particularities like a vacuum cleaner sucks up dust.

Ideas, beliefs, attitudes and emotional responses go into the personality bag along with minor gestures, oddments of speech and cultural trends. Some fragments are discarded while others stick. The mixture may coalesce into a coherent whole or not mix at all. A belief in the supernatural, absorbed by a toddler from a superstitious grandad might be completely at odds with

Beliefs

Attitudes

Emotional responses

estures

the habit of rational analysis instilled by a favourite teacher. The two attitudes get put in separate compartments – each one part of a different personality. When that toddler becomes an adult, the habit of rational analysis encouraged by the former teacher may become part of their major personality, but a visit to their grandparents' house may prompt the re-emergence of superstitions.

In rare cases, people experience severe personality switches, each personality having its own 'bag' of memories and knowledge that does not include awareness of the others. In one mindset a person may buy a full set of clothes which, in another state, they don't recognize.

Personality switches are associated with a phenomenon known as state-dependent memory. This refers to the way our brains privilege certain memories when we are in the same or similar state as when we had the original experience.

A classic experiment demonstrates this phenomenon. Volunteers were asked to memorize a string of words. Half had been given a stiff drink before the test. The next day, both groups were given alcohol before being asked to recall the words. The group who had been drunk when they memorized the words did more than twice as well as the group who had learned them while sober.

Like inebriation, personality is a state of mind. Autobiographical knowledge – who you are, where you live – is one part of that state and is usually very stable, while emotional responses and ways of behaving are other parts that vary in stability. Likes and dislikes tend to change according to circumstance, even in people who are otherwise very consistent.

FRAMES OF REFERENCE

Have you ever wondered why your friend reacts in one way, and you another? Or wished you could hold your cool like they do when anatagonized? The interesting thing about personalities is that we also associate them with acting differently. Once we recognize our different personalities, it becomes possible to learn from each different state.

A degree of changeability is a sign of flexibility – something that is increasingly needed to adapt to cultural shifts in our complicated, fast-changing world.

A multi-dimensional character may even protect you from illness. A research project conducted by psychologist Patricia Linville of Duke University in North Carolina, USA, suggests that the more of what she calls 'personality tributaries' or 'self-aspects' a person can identify with, the better equipped they are to weather stressful events.

Linville asked 100 college students to select characteristics such as 'outgoing', 'lazy' and 'affectionate' that they thought described themselves. She found that the more of these qualities that a student selected, and – importantly – the more distinctive they were from each other, the less likely the student was to suffer backaches, headaches, infections and menstrual cramps when they were under stress. They also reported fewer symptoms of depression.

Linville concluded that this was because a stressful event has less impact on a person who is aware of their multiplicity

because it affects only one, or some, of their personalities. As she puts it, 'A tennis player who has just lost an important match is likely to feel dejected, and these negative feelings are likely to become associated with this person's "tennis-player" self-aspect. But it won't spill over and colour the individual's other self-aspects if they are both numerous and distinct from one another. You have these uncontaminated areas of your life that act as buffers'.

As with 'major' personality testing, you can investigate minor personalities in yourself and others by thinking within a 'frame of reference'. Try putting yourself mentally into a particular role or situation, and answering questions from that perspective only. If you do the test as part of the selection procedure for a job, for example, you should answer the questions as though you are in the working environment. For instance, 'Do you become irritable if a person is late to meet you?' may be rephrased as, 'Would you issue a reprimand if an employee is late for a meeting without a good excuse?'

Recognizing your own minor personalities, and understanding what they are when you encounter them in others, will demystify some of the otherwise bewildering complexity of human behaviour and also provide you with strategies to tackle difficult situations. As with the 'tennis player' scenario, using a frame of reference can help you recognize how you might respond.

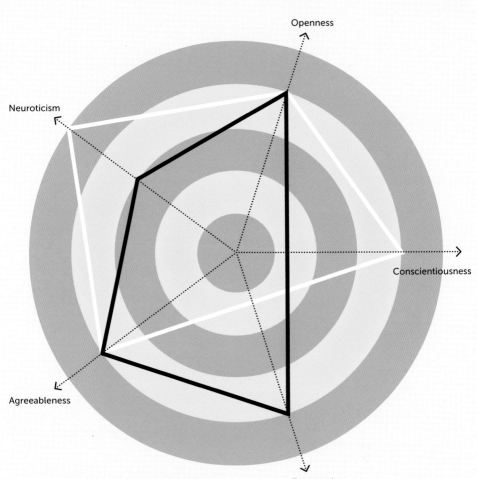

If you use different
frames of reference
when doing the quick
personality analysis in
Lesson 9, you may find
you display a different
personality in each one.
Here, the black line
delineates the shape
of a person's major
personality while they
were in their most

common state of mind.
The white line shows
the personality that
emerged when the
person retook the test
while 'framing' it in a
stressful work situation.
Their extroversion
was reduced, and
neuroticism and
conscientiousness
increased.

READING OTHERS' MINDS

Perhaps the most defining feature of human nature is our need for other people. There are practical reasons for this, of course; most societies are organized in such a way that we depend on each other to survive, either individually, or via social structures like commerce.

Our need for interaction with other people goes deeper than mere practicality. Very few of us could tolerate being entirely alone for a long period, even if our bodily needs were taken care of. Indeed, solitary confinement is one of the most dreaded punishments that can be meted out to a person. Research has shown that prisoners in solitary quickly become withdrawn, hypersensitive to sights and sounds, paranoid, and more prone to violence and hallucinations.

While personality trait and type analyses illuminate individual differences for purposes like job selection in our day-to-day lives, we need a more immediate way of knowing what is going on in other people's minds. We can never know that precisely, of course, but we do – literally – have an instinct for it.

In psychology, this is known as Theory of Mind (ToM). Put simply, it refers to the intuitive realization that other people have their own minds – a set of thoughts, feelings, intentions and judgements – that may be different from our own.

In most children, ToM emerges slowly in the first three or four years, along with the maturation of several areas of the brain. Together, the workings of these brain areas inform the child that they are an individual, and that their thoughts and feelings are

'inside' their heads rather than part of the outside world. Until that time, infants cannot clearly distinguish between their subjective world and the world outside.

As children make the distinction between their own minds and the rest of the world, they also start to understand that other people have feelings, emotions and a point of view that is different from theirs. Although we take it for granted, the conceptualizing required to have ToM is really quite complex. First you need to recognize yourself as something apart from the thoughts and perceptions that you are experiencing. You need to be able to remember the 'you' you were yesterday, with different thoughts and feelings, and imagine the 'you' you will be tomorrow. In this way, you start to recognize yourself as an object in the world (though a very special one), and one, furthermore, that you can look at as though from outside.

Once you have made that huge conceptual leap, you start to see that other objects in the world – the ones that are rather like you – also have worlds of private experience in their heads, just as you do in yours. This is ToM.

The emergence of ToM inevitably brings with it the sense of having an audience, and the ability to split ourselves into a private self (one that is known only to oneself) and a public self (one that can be observed and judged by its behaviour but not 'known' inside). In turn, that spawns yet another realization – we can deceive! The 'other' cannot know our thoughts or unobserved behaviour.

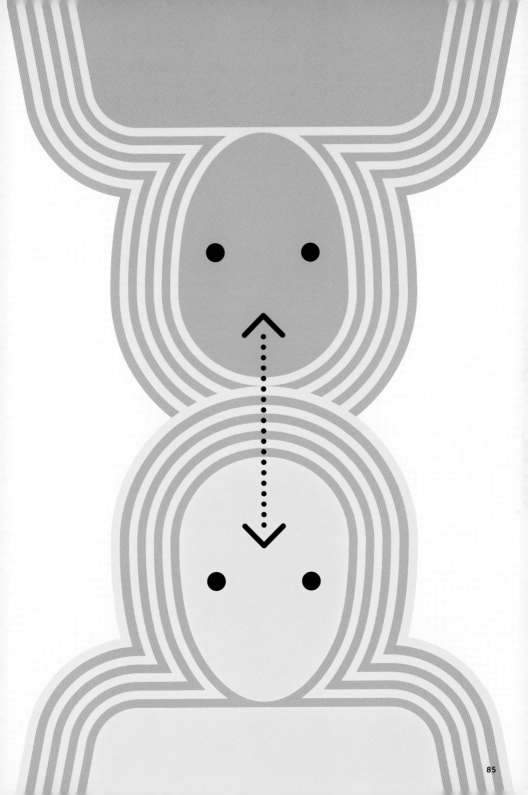

STEPPING INTO
ANOTHER'S SHOES

Zippo was Elizabeth's imaginary friend. He emerged when she was just three, and for about six months, any domestic mishap was Zippo's fault. Zippo knocked the vase off the table, pulled the cat's tail and ate the breakfast cereal that was later found under the table. Elizabeth's mother was less dismayed by Zippo's antics than by Elizabeth's new-found ability to tell rather obvious fibs.

Children start to tell lies – albeit rather clumsy ones – around the age of three. Their parents may be dismayed by it, but in fact they should take comfort from the fact that it shows their child's mind is developing the crucial ability to 'read' other minds.

ToM is closely associated (and possibly dependent on) another extraordinary brain function – the action of brain cells known as mirror neurons. Neurons generate the electrical currents that create our experiences and actions. For example, if a particular group of neurons fire, we will experience a pain in our right leg. Another group will produce a sensation of seeing red, another the thought of an apple, another the memory of an old friend, and so on.

Mirror neurons are special in that they fire both when we have a particular experience and when we see another person having that experience. Brain imaging studies have shown, for example, that a person watching another in pain will have activation in neurons that produce the pain in themselves.

The combination of ToM and mirror neurons go a long way towards bridging the gap between brains. They don't actually give telepathic access to another person's mind, but the effect is similar. The system is intuitive, but it can be enhanced. The first step is to acknowledge rather than to deny it.

The second step is to practise stepping (metaphorically) into the shoes of others and learning how it feels. Acting is exactly about this, but it tends to be something we think of as something that professionals do in order to entertain us, rather than a skill we should develop ourselves. However, acting, even badly, seems to enhance our ability to empathize and, by extension, to know what is happening in other people's minds. Researchers who gave children and adolescents a year of either acting training or other arts training (such as painting or music) found that the acting groups showed significantly better gains in empathy and ToM scores than the other groups.

The other technique shown to enhance this kind of 'mind-reading' is 'behavioural synchrony', which in simple terms is doing something in time with others, such as communal singing and dancing.

01 Child

02 Doll

One way to find out if ToM has developed in a child is to show them a model of a hilly landscape with a house in it, and place a puppet or doll in such a way that the doll would be unable to 'see' the house. The child is then positioned that the house is clearly visible to them but not to the doll, and is asked whether the other viewer (were they human!) can see it as well. Children who have developed ToM understand that although they can see the house, the doll has a different point of view – one in which the house is invisible. Before ToM has developed, they assume that if they can see the house, the doll can too.

TOOLKIT

09

Everyone is unique, but there are just five dimensions of behaviour: Openness to Experience, Conscientiousness, Extroversion, Agreeableness and Neuroticism. Between them, the Big Five dimensions encompass all possible personalities, and tests using this system can determine the exact 'shape' of any individual's personality. This is called 'trait analysis'.

10

A second way to describe an individual is by 'typing' them. Typology systems involve putting people into one of many categories. The scientific validation for type analysis is less rigid than for trait analysis, though it is very widely used in industry for staff selection.

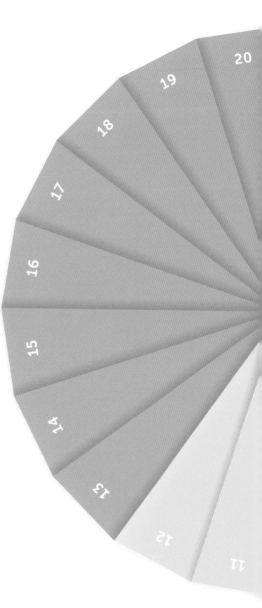

11

Few people have a single, consistent personality. Rather, we tend to jump from one personality to another according to the context. Recognizing these personality shifts, and cultivating changeability can help you to adapt to different situations.

12

Theory of Mind (ToM) is the automatic understanding that others have a separate sphere of consciousness, and that their feelings and thoughts are different from one's own. ToM promotes sympathy, empathy and learning through mimicry – it is a natural process that is learnt during childhood, and is a key process to understand as a parent.

FURTHER LEARNING

READ

Personality: What Makes You the Way You Are
Daniel Nettle
(Oxford University Press, 2009)

**Gifts Differing:
Understanding Personality Type**
Isabel Briggs Myers with Peter B. Myers
(Davies-Black, 2010)

**The People You Are:
The New Science of Personality**
Rita Carter
(Little, Brown, 2014)

Mindblindness: An Essay on Autism and Theory of Mind
Simon Baron-Cohen
(MIT Press, 1997)

WATCH

Theory of Mind
Uta Frith

Who are you, really? The puzzle of personality
Brian Little
TED Talk

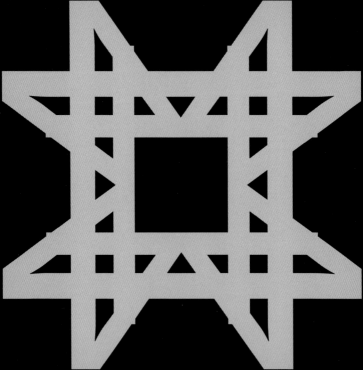

COMMUNICATION AND INFLUENCE

LESSONS

13 CONVERSATION FLOW
Reading between the lines of social interactions.

14 INSTINCT V INFLUENCE
The ancient art of persuading people to do what you would like.

15 CONFIDENCE
The advantages and down-sides of being sure of yourself.

16 MOVERS AND SHAKERS
The people who drive social movements.

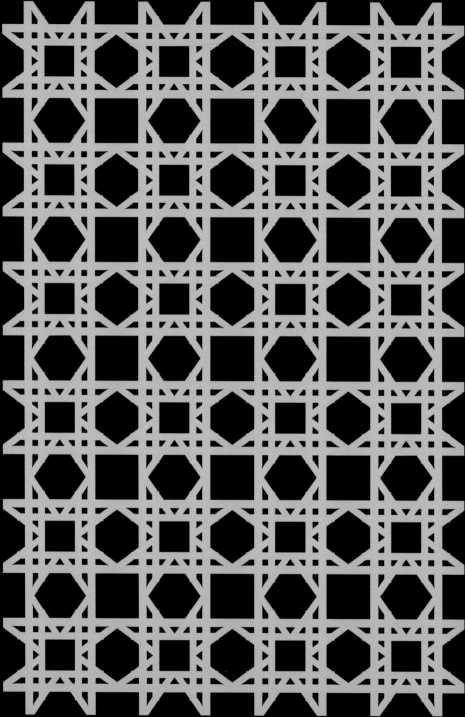

Mismatched acquaintances can walk away from each other when they don't get on, but when partners, co-workers or friends create a toxic form of interaction it can blight their lives.

Until now we have looked at people as individuals, considering how to read them in one-to-one situations. This chapter steps away to regard people in much the same way as an anthropologist might report on a newly discovered species.

Human beings excel in two areas: communication and imagination. Our unique ability to pass on knowledge through language, combined with the imagination to produce, between us, an infinite stream of new cultural ideas and artifacts makes us peculiarly diverse and unpredictable. Habits, customs, norms and values can spread via modern media at the speed of light and be adopted by millions of people overnight. The rich coating of culture we wear easily dizzies anyone trying to discern some essential human qualities beneath it.

However, when we strip away the surface behaviours, there are certain characteristics common to all human societies at all times. The most fundamental of these is our need to get together with others of our kind. To try to read people without considering their groups would be like trying to understand a bee without reference to the hive. This chapter examines the four main strata of human grouping: human society as a whole, the family, the group and crowds.

CONVERSATION FLOW

In 1965, when the Beatles were at their peak, they engineered a meeting with their idol Elvis Presley. The conversation did not flow and Elvis said, 'If you guys are just going to sit around looking at me, I'm going to bed'. The occasion was saved when the five got into a brief jam session. Later, though, John Lennon, disappointed by his hero, remarked, 'It was like meeting Engelbert Humperdinck'.

You've probably witnessed encounters like this, though probably not between superstars. You may even have organized one yourself – expecting friends to get on like a house on fire, only to find the meeting sputters out like a damp squib. Knowing people's individual personalities does not mean you can predict what happens when they meet, because their interaction is an entirely new creation.

Mismatched acquaintances can walk away from each other when they don't get on, but when partners, co-workers or friends create a toxic form of interaction it can blight their lives. Either the relationship fails and the people spring apart or they continue to be locked into a dysfunctional relationship. Sometimes the problem is a clash of personalities, ambitions or values, or the problem is a result of miscommunication and can be solved by analyzing how people speak to one another and making small changes in the way they respond.

This was the insight of psychologist Eric Berne who, in the 1950s, devised one of the most influential theories of social interaction – Transactional Analysis (TA). It is based on the recognition that most people develop an adult self, but within them lurks a bit of the parent, and a bit of the child.

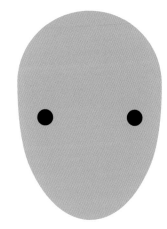

01. The adult deals with the reality of the here and now (it is the only ego state that is not connected to the past).

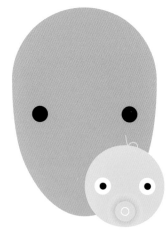

02. The parent thinks, feels and behaves as the person's parents or caregivers did in their childhood. A parent may be critical or nurturing.

03. The child plays back thoughts, feelings and behaviours that were experienced in childhood. They can be either Free or Adaptive.

All three 'selfs' are fine and can interact happily with others providing the person they are with responds in a complementary way. If the adult part of a person tries to communicate with the adult part of another person but gets a response from the parent part, or a child appeals to the parent and the adult 'self' responds, social interaction can quickly go very wrong.

Berne saw that basic social transactions – a single two-way exchange between individuals – come in two versions:

01. A complementary transaction is one in which person A says something from one ego state that invites person B to enter a complementary ego state. For example, if person A says, 'You look tired, I think you should go to bed', the statement comes from their parent ego and invites the child ego in person B to respond. Or if someone says, 'Ow! I've cut myself' (child ego state), the complementary response is, 'Here, let me put a plaster on it' (parent). Complementary transactions are Adult-Adult and Parent-Child, and vice versa.

02. Crossed or disconnected transactions occur when a person says something as a child or parent and is answered by an adult, or the adult speaks and gets a reply from a parent or child. For example, person A says, 'I'll get you something you like for supper' (parent), and B responds, 'Thanks, but I'll fix my own' (adult). When transactions are crossed, the conversation stalls. People may do it deliberately to cut communication with someone, or because they are angry.

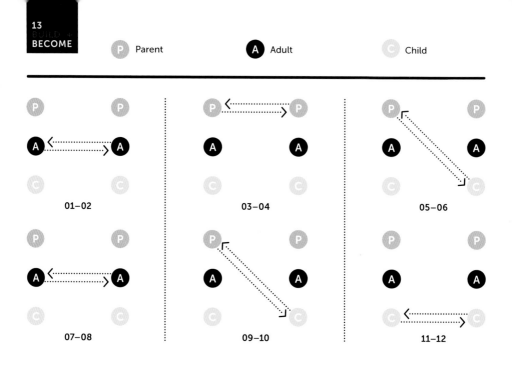

| | P Parent | A Adult | C Child |

RECOGNIZING EGO STATES

Listen carefully to any two people talking and the chances are you will start to discern the conversational dance of the parent/child/adult. Take this apparently straightforward 12-line conversation between a boss (B) and employee (E):

01B What time does the meeting begin?
02E Now, but the people from the legal department aren't here yet.
03B Typical!
04E Yes. They think they are a law unto themselves.
05B I have your report here – it's good but your grammar is terrible!
06E Oh, I'm sorry. I'll be more careful in future.
07B Ah! Here are the people from the legal department.
08E Good.
09B Here, come and sit next to me so you don't have to shout.

10E Thank you!
11B Oh look; they must have good news – they are carrying champagne!
12E Fantastic!

In this short exchange, both speakers switch effortlessly between ego states:

01 B speaks as an adult
02 E replies as an adult
03 Critical parent
04 Critical parent
05 Critical parent
06 Adaptive child
07 Adult
08 Adult
09 Nurturing parent
10 Adaptive child
11 Free child
12 Free child

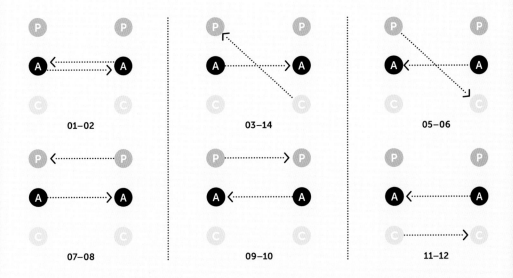

01–02	03–14	05–06	
07–08	09–10	11–12	

The conversation flowed just fine because, despite their ego switches, none of the transactions 'crossed' or disconnected. However, you only have to alter the conversation a tiny bit to have a different outcome. Say it goes like this:

01B What time does the meeting begin? (Adult)

02E Now, but the legal people aren't here yet. (Adult)

03B Well, they have had a lot to do. (Adult)

04E They are making me late for the next meeting. (Child)

05B I have your report here – it's good but the grammar is terrible! (Critical parent)

06E Does that matter? I had to do it quickly. (Adult)

07B Here are the people from the legal department. (Adult)

08E About time! (Critical parent)

09B Would you like to move nearer so you don't have to shout? (Nurturing parent)

10E I'm fine here if its OK with you. (Adult)

11B Oh look; they are carrying champagne! (Free child)

12E Rather early for me! (Adult)

Analyze this conversation and you see crossed or disconnected transactions all the way. The conversation is not acrimonious, but it fails completely to bring the two closer.

Obviously you can't analyze every little exchange in this way. But if you learn to recognize the parent, child and adult in yourself, you will soon find that you start to recognize it in others. Practise responding in a complementary way, and gradually it will become second nature.

INSTINCT V INFLUENCE

Seventy years after its first publication, Dale Carnegie's *How to Win Friends and Influence People* remains one of the bestselling books in the self-help market. Carnegie's advice – once you update the cosy examples – is practically indistinguishable from that to be found in millions of current self-help books and on websites.

This may be because the art of persuasion is unchanging and Carnegie just happened to write it down in a useful way before anyone else did. Alternatively, it may be that Carnegie's book and the hundreds that followed have influenced us to think that this is the way to deal with our fellow humans – make friends with them, then get them to do what we want.

You may feel there is something a little distasteful about the idea of linking friendship and influence, but there is no doubt it works. Getting another person to identify with you – a state that is implicit in friendship – makes it relatively easy to get them to bring their beliefs or attitudes closer to yours. If you can't quite pull off the friendship routine, you can do just as well in the influence stakes by inviting the other person to identify with someone they admire – a celebrity, for example.

Identification is not the only way to get people to do what you want, however. It is probably not even the most common. Directing people by influence as opposed to force is itself counter to many of our instincts. It is an indirect, cognitively complex way of achieving our aims, which probably only evolved when brute power and rigid social hierarchies gave way to more horizontally organized groups. The intuitive desire to dictate and/or to obey (usually both) remains in us all and still operates in many areas: politics, families with authoritarian heads, children in playgrounds, and countless workplaces with dominant bosses.

Compared to this, the gentle art of persuasion is obviously preferable. But it lies perilously close to psychological manipulation – a type of social influence that aims to change the behaviour or perception of others by deception. It is difficult to draw a clear demarcation between the two: is the salesperson's invitation to friendship, their solicitous enquiries about your health, the perceptive compliments, little personal admissions of error, and so on, manipulative and sinister or a genuine display of affinity? Does it even matter? Most of the time, perhaps, it doesn't. Friendship, even if feigned, oils the sticky business of human interaction and makes everyone feel better. But it is useful to know the difference.

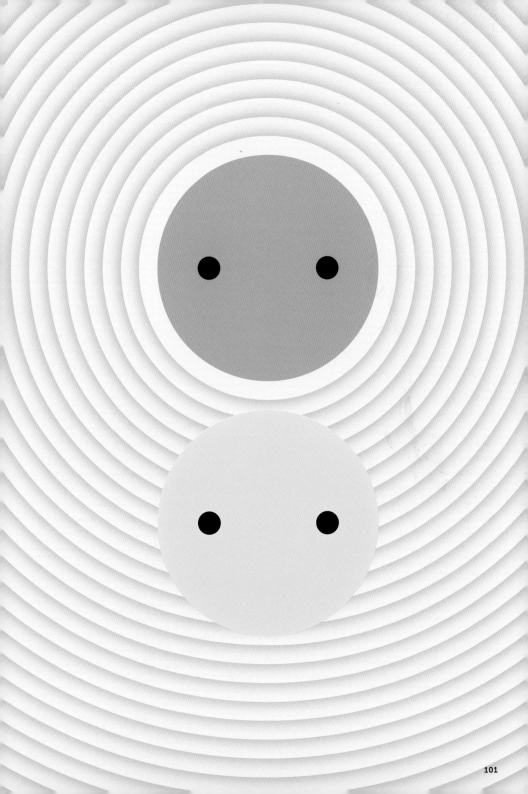

Reciprocity

PERSUASION

Charities regularly dispense free gifts with their written appeals – typically a few notelets and a pen. At first sight it seems wasteful, but charities consistently find that letters with gifts brings much more in donations than letters without gifts. Although people often report feeling uncomfortable about these unsolicited gifts, it seems that at least some of them nevertheless feel obliged or inspired to gift something back.

The charity gift tactic taps in to one of our deepest instincts: reciprocity. Given the chance, most babies will press a soggy piece of rusk or a flower petal on anyone who smiles at them – and the person who starts the friendly exchange of favours is likely to benefit most.

Robert Cialdini, generally considered to be the leading social scientist in the field of persuasion, identifies reciprocity as one of

the main weapons of influence. According to Cialdini, people are more open to your influence if they owe you for something you have done for them in the past. It is important, though, to make sure they have noticed your kindness. 'Don't say: "No big deal,"' says Cialadini. 'Label the act by saying something like, "No problem – that's what partners do for each other!"' This is what he calls 'prework'. When you subsequently need support for something, your act will be remembered as that of the 'partner' you are looking for now.

Commitment is another essential weapon, carefully lying beneath the sweet coating of persuasion. If you can get someone to agree to an idea or action, they are likely to honour it. 'Do You Sincerely Want to Be Rich?', asked the adverts for Bernie Cornfeld's dodgy pyramid selling outfit, IOS, in the 1960s.

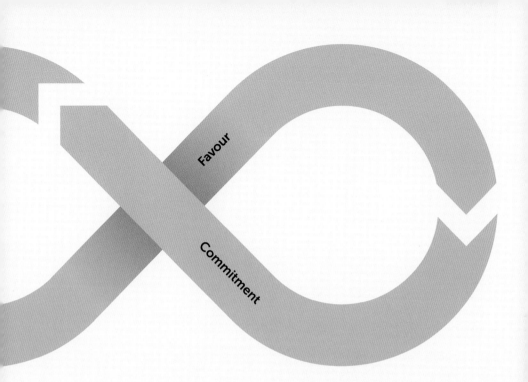

Favour

Commitment

Who could say 'no'? And how unreasonable would it be to say 'yes' and then refuse to hear the salesmen's pitch for attaining it. It's even better if you can convince a person to come up with the commitment themselves. If you want to persuade someone to join you in making a complaint in a restaurant, for instance, you might say, 'It's half an hour since we ordered. I wish there was something we could do.' Very often, the response will be, 'We could complain.'

Getting a person to commit publicly is especially powerful. The desire to be seen as consistent and reliable makes people very vulnerable to those who would like to take advantage of them. A telephone scam in 2015 separated thousands of people from the contents of their bank accounts. It involved a plausible-sounding person calling the 'target', claiming to be a member of their

bank's security department. The target was advised to move their money to a 'safe' account since their account was being tampered with by a criminal employee. This, they were told, would be an act of exemplary citizenship, for which they (the victim) had been specially selected due to their upstanding character and reliability (no mention was made of their fat bank balance).

Tricks like this have come to be known as confidence tricks, not because the perpetrators 'confide' anything, but because they depend on the victim's confidence – their belief in something or someone else. In con tricks, the confidence is, of course, sadly misplaced, but when it is internalized – that is, when the person has confidence in themselves – it can, as we'll see in Lesson 15, be remarkably powerful.

PEOPLE ARE
TO YOUR IN
IF THEY OW
SOMETHING
DONE FOR T

MORE OPEN
FLUENCE
E YOU FOR
YOU HAVE
HEM . . .

CONFIDENCE

I just typed 'How to boost your confidence' into Google and got 129 million results. 'How to boost your competence' only got one and a half million. Why are we apparently so much keener to enhance our confidence than our ability?

At first the answer seems obvious: high confidence is famously correlated with high social status, earnings and general success. The popular image of a confident person is someone who is 'comfortable' with themselves – someone with poise, charm and a calm assertiveness, free from the need to boast or put others down. Such an individual thinks positively, visualizes success, pushes their limits, looks on the bright side, has clear goals and so on. Of course we all want to be like that.

All these desirable qualities, however, are not actually confidence. In psychology, confidence means one thing: an individual's degree of certainty about their own capabilities, ideas and judgements in situations where these things cannot be accurately predicted. People who believe they are better than others are admired, listened to, promoted and feted more than others, whether or not they also possess charming qualities.

This would make sense if these people's beliefs were actually a reflection of their competence; it seems sensible to align ourselves with a winner in the hope that they will win for us too. But here's the funny thing: studies have shown that in simple tests of ability, the more confident a person is, the less good their performance.

The strange association between high confidence and low competence is known as the Dunning-Kruger effect after US psychologists David Dunning and Justin Kruger. In 1999, they discovered that certain particularly badly performing students considered themselves to be more competent than better-performing colleagues, even when contradictory results were clear to see. (Confident, incidentally, describes people who overestimate their capabilities by more than 30% – that being our baseline degree of confidence. As a species, we are predisposed to having unrealistically high self-confidence.)

In one experiment, a mixture of confident and underconfident people were invited to play a game together that involved finding their way around unknown territory. The most confident people quite soon became the leaders of the group and the others tended to adopt their ideas. The researchers thought this might be because the confident players put their ideas forward more forcefully. However, close observation showed that less confident players tended to go silent if an idea of theirs was rejected while confident players bounced back with more ideas.

On analysis, it was clear that both types had mismatched the real value of their ideas to their belief in their value. The confident people overvalued their ideas, while the underconfident players went the other way. Interestingly, it turned out that the confident people were the most wrong – if the team really had been exploring a virgin territory, it would have done better to follow those who were less sure of what they were doing.

A second self-serving illusion enables confident people to remain ignorant of their errors. When a task requires both skill (internal effect) and luck (external effect), confident people judge skill to have been the major determinant when they succeed, but think external factors – i.e. luck – are the main reason for their failures.

CHALLENGING CONFIDENCE

The effect of overconfidence permeates every bit of our lives. We are easily swayed by others' confidence, even when it is unjustified, and displays of confidence are given an inordinate amount of weight. Not only do people give confident types higher status, they also like them more than others.

Researcher Cameron Anderson from The University of California noted that after certain overconfident students in an experiment were shown to be bluffing, their classmates still thought they were terrific: 'The most overconfident people were considered the most beloved', he remarked. He subsequently analyzed the characteristic behaviour of the 'beloveds', and found their main distinction was that they participated more and were more relaxed – they genuinely believed in themselves. There was no faking it: 'People can soon spot the "tells" of false confidence,' says Anderson. 'If someone doesn't genuinely believe he is good, others pick up on his shifting eyes and rising voice.'

We might be attracted to it, but is high confidence really a good thing? It can be dangerous: it is probably responsible for a huge number of road accidents – 90% of drivers think they are above average – and economic disasters – a long-term study of professional financiers found they would do better if they had stayed in bed. In very real terms, confidence is a key factor in pay inequality between the sexes – men tend to think they are worth more, so they ask for more, and in return, tend to get more.

Professor Jeffrey Butler of the Einaudi Institute for Economics and Finance has suggested that the overconfidence of some perpetuates economic inequality on a global scale via a vicious circle. Overconfident people get privilege because they (falsely) believe they deserve it, and having achieved it, they view it as proof that they deserve it. Conversely, less confident people do not get privilege because they don't think they deserve it, and then take that failure as proof that they don't deserve it.

To test the idea, Butler took volunteers and randomly assigned them high or low pay to do a given task. There was no difference in competency between the high and the low paid, but those who received the low pay were 20% more likely to say they performed poorly than those who were better rewarded.

In view of this, should we really be pursuing those Google links to boost our confidence, or should we ask what we place our confidence in?

In a group, more confident individuals speak on behalf of the team. They make statements and use phrases indicating certainty, and express more certainty with others.

Less confident individuals speak only for themselves. They ask questions and express more agreement.

?

MOVERS
AND SHAKERS

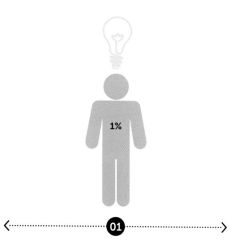

1%

←·· **01** ··→

Although the word 'fashion' is synonymous with clothes, every aspect of human life is subject to it. Most buildings can be dated to within a decade by their architectural style, old photos reveal hairstyles that make us cringe, and music, art, hobbies, sports, food, holiday destinations, university courses, and political and social movements come 'in' and go 'out' apparently regardless of their intrinsic value.

For something to become a trend, the environment must be right for it. An idea will only take off if it is promoted at the right time, if people are primed for it, and if the political and social mood is favourable. Trends tend to follow a five-stage process, driven by different types of people for different reasons.

01. Innovators develop new ideas and products for fun, money or because they see in them some social benefit. This tiny minority – maybe 1% or less of any population – are not primarily interested in trendsetting and for their ideas to catch on. For that they need to enthuse and engage other people.

02. Early adopters are the real trendsetters. They do not come up with novel ideas themselves but they are quick to spot and run with a good one. Their main driver is social status – they like to be thought of as leaders, movers and shakers, and often have a loud 'voice' in social networks and a reputation as an opinion setter or 'expert'. They ensure media publicity, celebrity take-up or, if appropriate, official adoption by public bodies. About 13% of people are early adopters.

03. Early majority These people are not style leaders and typically wait to see evidence that a new idea or product has value. They will nevertheless pick it up quicker than most people and promote it enthusiastically. About 34% of the population fall into this category, and their adoption of an idea signals the start of commercial frenzy (if it is a product) and globalization.

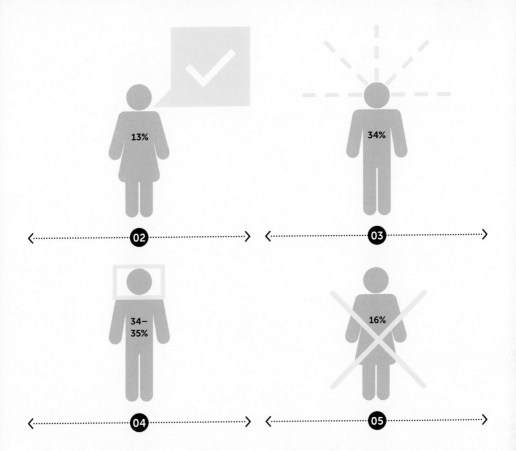

04. Late majority These people – hovering at the same 34–35% as the early majority – are conservative, scared of change, and wait for an idea or product to be thoroughly tried and tested before adopting it. They tend to be very conscious of social norms and anxious to stay safely within them. To appeal to them, novel ideas often need to be watered down.

05. Laggards About 16% of the population is bound by tradition and very conservative. These people actively fight against change and tend not to accept new things until they are no longer new. Once the laggards adopt an idea, it is a sure sign that something newer is already happening.

The people active at these five stages all reflect a different aspect of personality: inventiveness, a desire for social status, a tendency towards herding, an instinct for self-preservation and cautiousness. It is likely that the proportions of these types are fairly stable, and idea propagation was probably similar after the first human wrapped an animal skin around his feet and started a fashion for moccasins. What has changed, and is now changing dramatically, is the speed with which fashion spreads and passes through its cycles.

FAST FASHION

Do you remember low-rise trousers? This statement fashion piece of the 1960s was influenced by clothing in US prisons – where inmates were often prohibited from wearing a belt – and was worn by post-war youths looking to shake off the dreary dress of their parents. The power of celebrity brought these trousers into the mainstream with the likes of Janis Joplin and Jimi Hendrix turning them into a trend. The trend died totally in the 1970s, but two decades later it was back with Steve McQueen and supermodel Kate Moss.

The increasing speed of trend growth and death is due, of course, to better communications. When word travelled no faster than a horse, trends spread like moss rather than viruses. Gentlemen's wigs, for example, were first adopted by Louis XIV of France in 1580 as a means of disguising the follicular devastation of syphilis. The fashion spread through Europe, peaked about 100 years later, then died out over the next hundred.

Today, things move faster and further. Pokémon Go had 45 million users within two weeks of its launch, and even bizarre phenomena can spread into consciousness overnight – the 'Gangnam Style' YouTube video featuring a strange horseriding dance has been watched by more than three billion people.

WHO HAS INFLUENCE?

Trends today are increasingly started and maintained by social media sites. Viral marketing, also known as 'buzz marketing', occurs when people market to each other. This is rapidly taking over from traditional 'top-down' marketing. Facebook, for example, currently has more than two billion active users, each of whom spends an average of 50 minutes every day on the site. The potential for trendsetting offered by Facebook and other social media sites is enormous, and has allowed the first important stage of the trendsetting process – the 'early adopter' phase – to be controlled much more easily.

Fashion news is often broken on Facebook and Twitter, bloggers are consulted by fashion 'bibles' such as Vogue and fashion designers are live-streaming their shows.

The average Facebook users has about 350 online 'friends' . If just one in five of them comments or even just 'likes' something, this means that more than 3,000 other users may be alerted within minutes. Understanding who is behind the likes becomes important – influencing can only really take off if you are influencing the right audience.

Researchers sampled patterns of behaviour among 1.3 million Facebook users to identify those who were most likely to influence others to adopt a new product. They found that younger users are more susceptible to influence than older users, men are more influential than women, women influence men more than they influence other women, and married individuals are the least susceptible to influence.

Some trends grow by word of mouth, while others are launched by powerful social influencers, such as governments, Hollywood or the fashion industry. The growth pattern is different for each, although large organizations increasingly use 'bottom-up' tactics such as getting well-connected individuals or celebrities to promote an idea or product to all their friends.

Top-down trend

01. Typical top-down trend showing a steep rise in adopters immediately after launch.

Preference trend

02. Here, the trend is driven by people's preferences only. Its popularity branches out among the people who are making the choices and the rise in popularity starts slowly – person #1 tells a few friends, then each of those people tells a few friends. As a proportion of the entire population, each person has a relatively small number of friends; but at some point, the growth can accelerate rapidly. Suppose each person has five friends. At the first stage, only six people are involved (1 + 5); stage two adds another 25, stage three another 125, and so on. The idea 'catches on.'

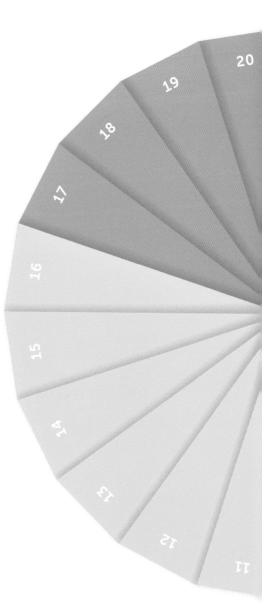

TOOLKIT

13

People usually slip between different ego states most commonly child, parent and adult. Successful conversations depend on adult-to-adult or parent-child exchanges. Recognizing these exchanges can help you build better dynamics.

14

People are more likely to comply with another's wishes if they are encouraged to feel they owe the other person something, and that they are committed to doing or giving it.

15

The hallmarks of confidence are relaxation and social engagement. These traits generate a display of knowledge that people are attracted to and trust in.

16

New inventions or discoveries take off when they are taken up by 'early adopters' – people who are central to a network of influential friends. Recognizing early adopters can be key in pioneering your ideas.

FURTHER LEARNING

READ

Games People Play: The Psychology of Human Relationships
Eric Berne (Penguin, 1973)

How to Win Friends and Influence People
Dale Carnegie (Vermilion, 2006)

Overconfidence and War: The Havoc and Glory of Positive Illusions
Dominic Johnson
(Harvard University Press, 2009)

Climbing the Charts: What Radio Airplay Tells Us About the Diffusion of Innovation
Gabriel Rossman
(Princeton University Press, 2012)

Win Bigly: Persuasion in a World Where Facts Don't Matter
Scott Adams
(Penguin, 2017)

The Persuaders: The Hidden Industry That Wants to Change Your Mind
James Garvey
(Canongate Books, 2017)

Decoded: The Science Behind Why We Buy
Phil Barden
(John Wiley & Sons, 2013)

WATCH

Wall Street

The Wolf of Wall Street

CARM: The Conversation Analytic Role-play Method
Professor Elizabeth Stokoe
http://www.carmtraining.org/

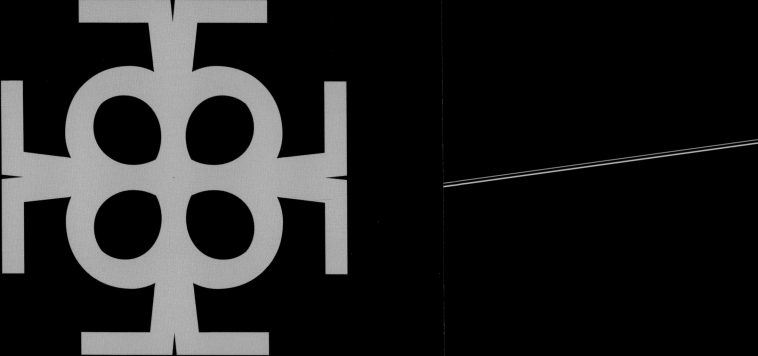

READING SOCIETY

LESSONS

17 GROUPS
Human beings have evolved for group living, but the group needs to be the right size.

18 FAMILIES
Families are held together by a chemical.

19 GROUPTHINK
Why groups sometimes make worse errors than individuals.

20 CROWDS
What turns a peaceful gathering into a frightening mob?

To try to read people without regard to their societies would be like trying to understand a bee without reference to the hive.

Until now we have looked at people as individuals, considering how to read them in one-to-one situations. This chapter steps away from the individual to look at people *en masse*. We learn to start reading others like an anthropologist – in context, and as a part of groups and societies.

Human beings excel in two areas: communication and imagination. We have a unique ability to pass on knowledge through language. This, combined with the imagination to produce an infinite stream of new cultural ideas and artifacts, makes us peculiarly diverse and unpredictable. Habits, customs, norms and values can spread via modern media at the speed of light and become adopted by millions of people overnight. The rich coating of culture we wear easily dizzies anyone trying to discern some essential human qualities beneath it.

When we strip away the surface behaviours, however, there are certain characteristics that are common to all human societies at all times. The most fundamental of these is our need to get together with others of our kind. To try to read people without regard to their societies would be like trying to understand a bee without reference to the hive.

This chapter examines the four main strata of human grouping: human society as a whole, crowds, groups and the family.

GROUPS

All people have certain basic needs that can't be met by the individual alone. People need people and the structure of human society reflects this. Everyone is part of a group, the group in turn is invariably part of a larger group, which is part of a still larger group.

Like clouds in a windy sky, human groups constantly form, break up and reform. A few fly high and are clearly bounded, while others are wispy and short-lived. Even the biggest may suddenly fall apart (empires), while the smallest may persist for centuries (the European aristocracy). There are huge groups based on geography and those based on beliefs; groups bound by common interests, such as farming or sports; groups bound by race, or blood or age; and tiny groups that form in close environments, such as neighourhood gangs or book clubs.

The needs that stop us drifting off alone were charted, famously, in a five-layer pyramid drawn up by the American psychologist Abraham Maslow. He described our foundational needs (identical for every living thing) as physiological: air to breathe, food and water – the basics for survival. Above these is safety: the things we need to secure our long-term survival such as shelter and protection from foes. Next up are social needs: the love of family, support of friends and a sense of being embedded in society. After that, there is self-esteem: the desire to be respected, both by ourselves and others. And finally, at the pinnacle, there is what

Maslow described as self-actualization: the drive to fulfil ourselves as human beings – whether this means satisfying inventiveness or creativity, seeking spiritual growth, intellectual exploration, or just attaining a sense of contentment.

All but the least fortunate manage to satisfy the basic needs for survival, but very few of us are at the glorious pinnacle of self-actualization (Maslow himself calculated it was only one in 10). Most people are in the middle 'social' layers of the pyramid.

Maslow drew up his hierarchy in 1943, but it has rarely been tested objectively. In 2011, however, University of Illinois researchers scrutinized data collected over five years from over 150 countries. It included surveys of people's feelings matched to the extent to which they had attained Maslow's needs. The researchers found his theory was broadly correct; in cultures all over the world, the fulfilment of a person's basic needs for survival and safety correlated with their happiness. However, the research showed something more: the two middle needs – social inclusion and respect – correlated with a jump in satisfaction from mere happiness to 'joy'. In other words, being safe and secure makes us happy, but doing things with other people makes us *really* happy. Maybe that is why so few people move on to self-actualization – we are more interested in hanging out with the crowd.

SELF-ACTUALIZATION

SELF-ESTEEM

BELONGING

SAFETY

PHYSIOLOGICAL NEEDS

THE RULE OF 150

Generally, the higher a species is in the food chain, the less its members need to stick together. Apex predators – animals that have no natural predators like sharks – tend to be loners. By contrast, animals that are constantly at risk of becoming someone else's dinner usually live in herds or flocks.

People are tricky to place in the food chain. Our technological prowess has effectively made us apex predators, but if you remove our armaments, we slither right down the chain. We may preen like a tiger when we are puffed up by our war tools, or flock like sheep when we are naked and afraid.

There is a third type of group that suits people very well – the pack.

Packs are different from herds. In a herd, each individual obeys one simple rule: 'run when the others run'. By contrast, packs form goals and individuals interact with each other to attain them, configuring their place in the group: 'I run when that one runs but hold back if the other one runs – unless that one is holding back too.' It's a bit like sport – in football, there is the overall plan of winning the game, while each individual is charged with striking or saving a goal and has to work with the others to do it.

Given the complications of working in a pack, it helps a great deal if you know the people you are with. Every one of these social connections is encoded in a person as a pattern of electrical activity in their brain. These patterns run on physical 'wiring', which is sustained by neurons in the neocortex – evolutionarily the most recent area of the brain. The number of detailed relationships an individual can sustain is therefore limited by the complexity and extent of their neural wiring. Human beings have a large neocortex compared to other animals, but it cannot cope with an infinite amount of social information.

This limit to our social cognition dictates the maximum size of the pack we can maintain as a stable unit. It seems be about 150 people. This number has become known as Dunbar's number, after the Oxford anthropologist Robin Dunbar. He arrived at it by applying the social brain theory, which holds that the size of primate social groups is directly related to the size of their brains. Using information on both primates and the average size of the human neocortex, he calculated his number, then checked it against the size of real human groups finding many matches: 150 is about the average number of people living in villages untouched by social engineering, and roughly the size of military units through the ages.

The 'Rule of 150' is now used widely in business management. Even before Dunbar's study, the US manufacturer of Gore-Tex found, through trial and error, that when a manufacturing unit reached 150 employees, it was best not to expand it any further but to start a new unit elsewhere. Since then, the technique of breaking companies into working sections of 150 or less is fairly common – it means that everyone is able to know their colleagues' names and management can be exercised without a strong hierarchical, and therefore divisive, structure.

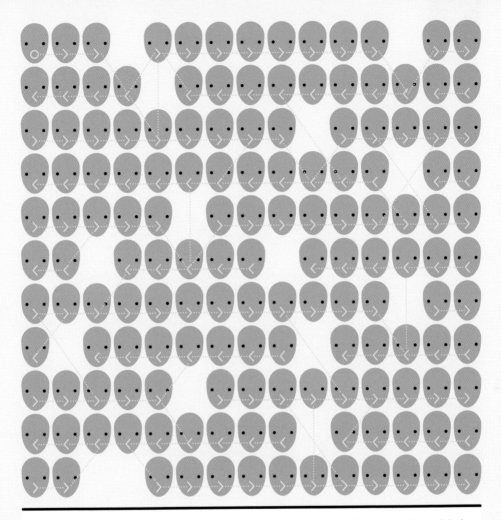

It is worth noting that 150 is the maximum group size that Dunbar calculated we can maintain, not the optimum. Primates maintain their social connections by grooming each other and the larger the group size, the more time they spend picking insects out of each others' fur. The human equivalent is gossip. When Dunbar calculated the proportion of their time that members of a human group of 150 would need to spend keeping tabs on each other, he came up with 42%. A 2014 survey of 3,000 workers across a variety of industries found that this is precisely the amount of time that people in offices spent gossiping.

FAMILIES

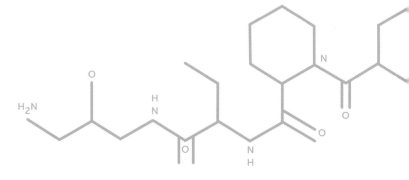

The family, in one form or another, is the most basic grouping in every society. Whether it consists of a rambling cluster of vaguely related people or a tight, nuclear household, practically everyone has a family, and was raised in one.

The universality of the family reflects humans' primeval need to form protective bonds. Unlike some other species, human infants are born helpless, so over the ages we have evolved a powerful mechanism for keeping offspring close to their mothers. Given that the baby's mother needs protection too, the same mechanism encourages blood relatives to form a close and mutually protective group. Sometimes

it draws friends, even pets, into the magic circle. The mechanism is basically chemical – a hormone called oxytocin.

Although it is 'just' a chemical, oxytocin can plausibly be regarded as the architect of the family. Known popularly as the 'cuddle' hormone, oxytocin is produced in the brain whenever people feel close, and particularly when they express this through physical affection. It is released during sex and childbirth, and thereafter every time the mother and baby touch. Stroking and caressing someone you love elevates oxytocin levels, which in turn lowers stress hormones and reduces blood pressure. It even works when the affection is towards

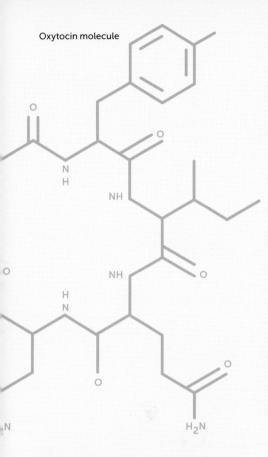

Oxytocin molecule

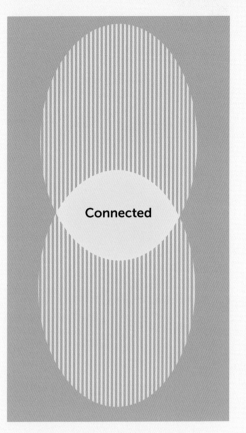

Connected

a pet animal – and the effect on the pet is similar to that seen in people!

One of the things oxytocin does in the brain is to disrupt normal awareness of our body's boundaries. When people are high on oxytocin – after making love, for example – it is common for them to feel as though they have 'merged' with each other into a single, warm being.

It is what happens when oxytocin levels fall, however, that makes human bonding so effective.

Helpless though human babies are, they have their tricks: as soon as their oxytocin levels fall (which happens whenever they are not being actively cared for), they produce what psychologists call 'social releaser' behaviours. The most obvious is crying. The effect of this very particular sound is to send the caregiver flying to the baby to give it comfort and/or food. Once the two are together, the baby's oxytocin levels rise, along with the parent's. So long as the two remain in this warm hormonal bath they feel calm, but as soon as they separate, their oxytocin levels start falling again and the plunge can only be reversed by resuming contact. A similar effect occurs when adults fall in love. The pattern oxytocin creates – chemical 'high' from contact, followed by 'craving' while apart, followed by the 'fix' of reunion – is identical to a drug addiction.

ATTACHMENT STYLES

Short of becoming addicted, promoting oxytocin release through affection is good for your relationships, stress levels and possibly your health. Some studies have found that oxytocin speeds wound healing. It can even make you look more attractive – though only in the eyes of your partner! One study found that artificially elevated oxytocin levels in men made them fancy their partners more, and actually put them off other women.

The most important function of oxytocin, however, is to endow infants with a sense of security that will provide them with a solid emotional foundation for life. The oxytocin-conducted duet between parent and child ensures that the child has at least one reliable attachment – a person they can depend on to meet their needs.

According to the late John Bowlby, the foremost authority on human attachment, when a child's initial bonding experience goes to nature's plan, it creates in them an internal 'working model' of society. The model consists of three convictions:

01. That people are trustworthy.
02. That they (the infant) themselves have value.
03. That they can exert an effect on others.

If this model is not properly formed, it will undermine the child's social and emotional behaviour thereafter. Bowlby's colleague, psychiatrist Mary Ainsworth, subsequently described three distinct types of attachment:

> Secure
> Anxious-resistant
> Anxious-avoidant

She arrived at these descriptions by placing one-year-old children in a strange place and then briefly separating them from their mother or caregiver. Secure children (the majority) became upset when they were left but were happily reunited and easily comforted when the mother came back. Anxious-resistant children (about one in five) became extremely distressed during separation, but were difficult to soothe when the parent came back and seemed angry, as though they wanted to punish the parent for leaving. Anxious-avoidant children didn't appear too distressed by the separation, but, upon reunion, actively avoided contact with their parent, sometimes turning their attention to play objects.

These patterns of attachment seem to stick for life. Secure babies grow into secure adults, able to form healthy relationships based on trust. Anxious-resistant babies are prone to being clingy or jealous adults, desperate for contact but angry at their own need. Avoidant babies find attachment much harder, and often feel distant.

Attachment styles have also been linked to people's behaviour in business. They influence whether managers have close or distant relationships with the people who report to them, communicate directly or indirectly, micromanage or empower, encourage debates or shut them down.

The oxytocin system is a brilliantly effective way of maintaining strong links between people. If it goes wrong, the effects can reverberate through generations. Happily, people who find bonding difficult because of their own upbringing can prevent passing on their misfortune to their offspring by 'faking' normal bonding – a process that ultimately helps them too.

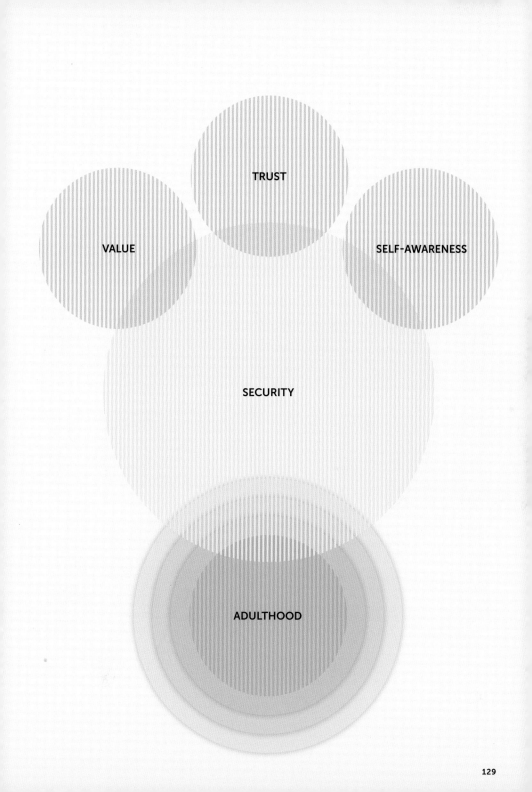

VALUE

TRUST

SELF-AWARENESS

SECURITY

ADULTHOOD

PEOPLE ARE
BEING IN A
GROUP GIVE
A NICE WAR

SOCIAL AND
COHESIVE
S A PERSON
M FEELING.

GROUPTHINK

In April 1961, President John Kennedy ordered the mighty force of the US military to invade Cuba. They expected to wrest power from its communist leader, Fidel Castro, much as an adult might take a rattle from a baby. Three days later, it was all over, but not quite as Kennedy's team had predicted. Instead of triumph, America was sent scurrying by the Cubans. The Bay of Pigs invasion was one of military history's most notorious miscalculations.

Subsequent analysis suggests the root cause of the fiasco was 'groupthink' – the failure of a group to allow independent or critical thought to sully consensus. Kennedy's team accepted without question the invasion plan from the CIA, who themselves seem to have neglected some glaring problems with it. The team then buoyed each other up to create what turned out to be an unreal expectation of success. Those within the team who harboured misgivings conformed to the majority opinion and outside experts were ignored or dismissed. Groupthink paved the road to disaster.

The term groupthink was coined in 1952 by writer William H. Whyte who likened it to something from Newspeak in George Orwell's *1984*. It was not mere conformity, he wrote, but 'rationalized conformity – an open, articulate philosophy, which holds that group values are not only expedient but right and good as well.'

Groupthink occurs when people want very badly to agree with each other. This is more common than not, because – as we have seen – people are fundamentally social and being in a cohesive group gives a person a nice, warm feeling.

The feeling is not unlike like that of a mother bonding with her baby, and this is no coincidence. The biological mechanism that creates the mother/child bond – the hormone oxytocin – is probably one of the main culprits in creating groupthink. Studies have shown that the hormone promotes close teamwork in sports and business, and quickly builds loyalty between people who are told they are on the same side. It encourages people to trust one another, empathize, share, and assist.

Oxytocin has a dark side, however. It also creates distrust (possibly even hatred) of people outside the group. And in some situations it provokes envy, pleasure in others' misfortune and aggression.

It follows that once you are on the inside of a group glued together by oxytocin, you really do not want to be pushed outside. If the price of staying in favour with co-bondees is to stop thinking critically, most people, it seems, find it easy to pay.

Bound together in their agreeable huddle, group members typically avoid anything that might disturb their serenity. The group isolates itself from critical outsiders and engages in self-congratulatory rhetoric. There is a dangerous tendency for the group to overrate its own powers and underrate its competitors.

Psychiatrist Solomon Asch gave the clearest ever demonstration of groupthink in a series of experiments in the 1950s. In a typical experiment, he would gather eight people in a room, seven of whom were stooges, while just one was the real subject of the experiment. That person was led to believe that the others were also volunteers. Asch lined up the group and asked them, one by one, to judge which of a number of lines was longest.

The 'real' volunteer would be at the end of the line. The seven stooges gave obviously wrong answers – 1, for example, or 3. The question the experiment set out to answer was:
What would the eighth person say?

Over the series, about 30% of volunteers joined the stooges in giving a false answer. Afterwards, when they were told what had happened, they offered one of three explanations:

01. They genuinely saw the line lengths as they judged.

02. They saw the real answer but thought it must be wrong because everyone else saw it differently.

03. They knew their answer was wrong, but agreed with the others because they feared being the odd man out.

Asch's experiment has been replicated hundreds of times throughout the world, with similar results. However, the proportion of people who conform to the group differs considerably – from about 15% to 58% according to culture. People from cultures that celebrate individualism (such as the USA or western Europe) were more likely to give the correct answer despite the group pressure, while those from traditionally collective societies, (such as Japan and India) were more likely to conform.

ILLUSION OF INVULNERABILITY

One of the most obvious danger signs of groupthink is when a group starts to issue self-aggrandizing publicity. It may begin as a conscious attempt to make people outside the group think that the group is better than they are. A small company, for example, might put out advertising that suggests they are much bigger than they are, in the rational hope of attracting business that might otherwise go to a larger competitor. The rot sets in when the group (or company) start to believe their own bigged-up claims.

Researcher Jack Eaton noted the role of media manipulation in the economic plunge experienced by UK retail giant Marks and Spencer in the late 1990s. The company issued press releases that produced acres of positive coverage associating it with national pride and supremacy. Those most convinced by the publicity seem to have been the board members themselves, who Eaton claim, developed an 'illusion of invulnerability'. Their

self-belief led them to launch a disastrous expansion strategy, which ended with the price of company shares plummeting from 590 to less than 300 in one year.

Groupthink has been most frequently identified and analyzed in cases where it has led to catastrophe on a grand scale, but the phenomenon is as common around the supper table as in the boardroom. Whenever a handful of people come together with good intentions and a common goal, groupthink is liable to set in. If the goal is trivial – to select a bottle of wine from the menu or navigate the best route home – it may not seem to matter; keeping a happy consensus is probably worth drinking a dodgy wine or spending 10 minutes in a traffic jam. But agreement 'for a pleasant life' can too easily become a habit that prevails when the goal does matter. Indeed, the more pleasant group life is, the greater the risk of groupthink and potentially awful consequences.

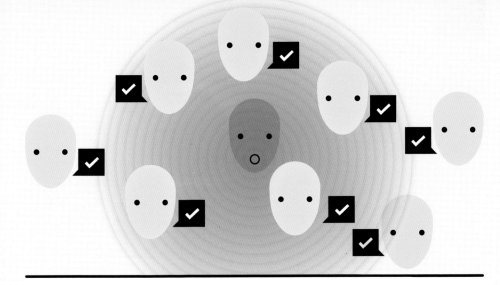

HOW TO GUARD AGAINST GROUPTHINK

01. Be suspicious of exaggerated agreeableness and mutual admiration within the group. Note how much nodding goes on when other people are talking and count the number of times people congratulate each other. Is it more than in normal conversation?

02. Note external stressors — this is when the group's need to bond closely is at its highest and people are least likely to say or do anything disruptive.

03. If you are a group leader, hold back on your own opinion until others have spoken. Groupthink is especially likely to occur in groups with a leader who states their own opinions first.

04. Discourage excessive respect for authority.

05. Talk to group members outside group gatherings — criticisms are more likely to be voiced when the fear of communal disagreement is reduced.

06. Say something different that goes against the consensus — the chances are that it will free someone else to speak up, and debate can then begin.

07. Bring in people who are not natural members of the group and who do not particularly want to be part of it. Their perspective will be different and they will care less about being pushed out if they disagree with the mainstream.

08. Invite experts from outside to address the group and encourage members to do their own research and not depend on shared sources of information.

09. If the group is large enough and the project long enough, form a sub-committee to bring recommendations back to the group. Even two people will get a better hearing than a lone voice.

CROWDS

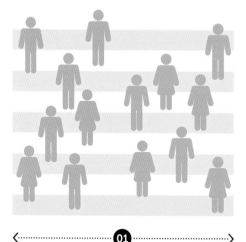

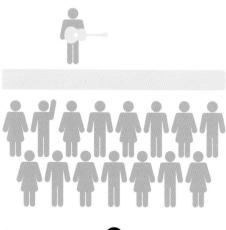

<------------- **01** -------------> <------------- **02** ------------->

Getting 'caught up' in a crowd can be joyous or terrifying. Joyous if you are waving your mobile phone in the air at a concert or dancing behind a float at a carnival; terrifying if you find yourself stumbling along in a press of people fleeing from a fire or kettled with frustrated protestors at a demonstration.

Emotions are amplified in a crowd, and extreme behaviour can emerge. You might even find yourself doing things that, alone, you would not contemplate. Sometimes it seems as though the crowd is an entity quite separate from those within it.

The idea of a 'group mind' was first formally proposed by French polymath Gustave le Bon in his 1895 work *The Crowd: A Study of the Popular Mind*. According to Le Bon, the individual within a crowd '... is no longer himself but has become an automation who has ceased to be guided by his will... [He possesses] ... the spontaneity, the violence, the ferocity

and also the enthusiasm and heroism of a primitive being'.

Since then, the dynamics of collective behaviour have been greatly refined and it is now known that it takes several factors to produce the 'primitive' entity Le Bon describes. There are several different types of crowds and each exhibit different behaviours.

01. Casual crowds are large numbers of people who happen to be in the same place at the same time. They do not identify as a crowd and are not particularly aware of being a component part, although (unrealized by most) quite sophisticated collective behaviour may be at work. Pedestrians using a busy pavement, for example, obey quite complex rules in order not to collide.

02. Conventional crowds are brought together by a central attraction – a film or concert – but being part of a crowd is not

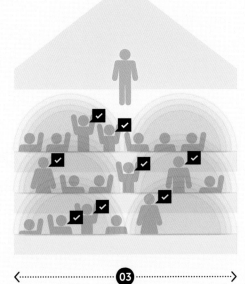

03

04

the focus. The members are more or less neutral towards one another, and communal emotional expression is not generally part of the deal – though it may show itself as applause or other 'conventional' audience behaviour. Attendees do not have a common aim beyond the event, dispersing once it has finished.

03. Expressive crowds consist of people who are gathered primarily to express one or more emotions that they hold in common. Although they often gather around some central attraction or event, such as a religious meeting, the main motivation for most participants is to be part of the crowd; without it the event would be pointless. Members want to express their feelings in a context of agreement: to cheer, clap or chant. The emotions generated are generally positive and life-affirming, even when the purpose of the crowd is to protest.

04. Active crowds gather with intent to be the event. Flash mobs, for example, are large groups of people who assemble suddenly in a public place to perform – they are organized in advance, yet have no other connection to one another.

More commonly, active crowds are brought together to protest, or to combat something they dislike – perhaps a political rally or mass demonstration. Active crowds tend to be in an emotionally roused state even before they have formed.

Apart from the active-aggressive crowd, most crowds form, enjoy whatever it is they gathered for, and disperse: there is nothing inherently unstable or threatening about them. However, given certain circumstances, people *en masse* are vulnerable to sudden and extreme changes of mood and behaviour.

CROWD CONTAGION

In 1963, shortly after the Beatles topped the pop charts for the first time, they were booked by promoter Andi Lothian to play at the Glasgow Odeon. As they came on stage, the audience erupted in what Lothian described as, 'absolute pandemonium. The whole hall went into some kind of state almost like collective hypnotism.'

Since then, 'Beatlemania-style' behaviour has become an accepted norm at certain events. Yet even the most ardent fan would hesitate to scream and shout if they were watching a performance alone.

The transformation from a peaceable gathering to a frenetic mob occurs when two or more of the following conditions apply:
> Emotions are whipped up.
> There is an external threat or peril (rumoured or real).
> There is externally applied antagonism or opposition.
> Mimicking – one person in a crowd does something extraordinary and others copy it, assuming it is 'normal' for the situation.

These conditions tap into our emotions, and when ramped up can run through a crowd at lightning speed – especially if the participants in it are already primed. This effect, known as contagion, is probably due to our brain's mirror neurons (see page 86), which transmit feelings faster than words. Contagion is a powerful survival technique, and is quick to activate.

Emotion is frequently exploited in scenarios such as rallies that naturally have large numbers of attendees, to encourage the formation of a collective identity. For example, in political campaigns, candidates often create a sense that there is a common threat, seeking to unite people through emotions such as fear or resentment and consequently, position themselves as the solution.

Crowds often seem to behave dangerously and erratically, but within the collective entity there is also wisdom. In some circumstances, a mass of people exhibits more intelligent behaviour than even the smartest individual member. Indeed, if one person in a group erroneously appears to have greater knowledge of the subject and others go along with their ideas, greater error occurs as the mistakes they make are amplified.

If, however, the people in a crowd are very different from one another, with different sources of information, and do not get together to form a group opinion, there is a benefit. Experiments run by the Swiss Federal Institute of Technology found that when a group of people was asked a question they could not accurately answer, such as the precise length of a river, the range of their answers got narrower when they discussed the question, and all their answers tended to be wide of the mark. If the individuals did not talk together but just guessed individually, the range of answers was wider but the centre of the range was usually fairly accurate.

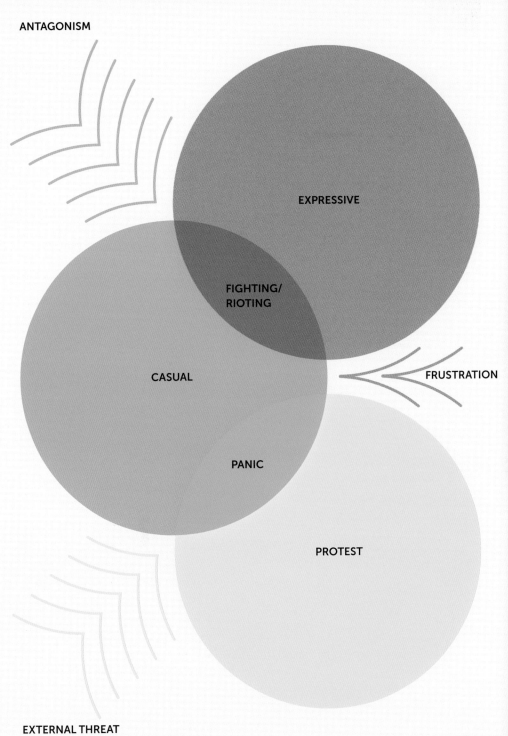

ANTAGONISM

EXPRESSIVE

FIGHTING/
RIOTING

CASUAL

FRUSTRATION

PANIC

PROTEST

EXTERNAL THREAT

TOOLKIT

17

Human groups are limited in size by the number of relationships that each person can handle. One way the group is kept connected is by gossip, the equivalent of grooming in other primates. These connections help us to ascertain behaviour and, in some instances, influence it.

18

Families are the tightest of social groups, and they are found all over the world. The glue that binds close relatives is a hormone and neurotransmitter called oxytocin, which rises when a person is near their loved ones and drops when they are separated. High levels produce a sense of warmth and security, so it automatically keeps families bonded.

20
19
18
17
16
15
14
13
12
11

19

Our need to be within a group is so strong that we regularly alter our perceptions and opinions to fit in with the majority. This is known as 'groupthink' and when it happens in important situations – such as when military or policy decisions are being made – it can be disastrous.

20

Crowds can turn into mobs if certain factors are in place. The crowd needs to be emotionally roused, challenged, and to contain amongst it certain individuals who exhibit extreme behaviours that others mimic. Understanding crowd behaviour is critical in anticipating behaviour.

FURTHER LEARNING

READ

How Many Friends Does One Person Need?
Robin Dunbar (Faber & Faber, 2011)

The Human Story
Robin Dunbar (Faber & Faber, 2004)

The Hormone of Closeness: The Role of Oxytocin in Relationships
Kerstin Uvnäs-Moberg (Pinter & Martin, 2013)

The Child, the Family, and the Outside World
D.W Winnicot (Penguin, 2000)

The Power of Others
Michael Bond (Oneworld, 2014)

The Crowd: A Study of the Popular Mind
Gustave le Bon (Sparkling Books, 2009)

WATCH

Twelve Angry Men
This classic film shows how groupthink can lead people to a disastrous conclusion – and how individuals can be made to see the light by one clear-thinking person.

STUDY

www.study.com/academy/lesson/group-think-definition-examples.html
Try this online course dedicated to groupthink.

EPILOGUE

There are 7.5 billion people in the world, every one of them with their own ambitions, desires, history and opinions. Yet we all inhabit a similar sort of body with similar needs, evolved to perceive the world in a similar way. Our shared biology, and the psychological imperatives that spring from it (such as the need for security and love), give us a starting point for shared understanding.

In this book, I have tried to keep our biological commonality in sight in order to provide a sketch – much like an architect's first drawing – of the main struts of human behaviour. It emphasizes the ways in which we are similar, rather than the things that set us apart.

Knowing about people in general, however, is not necessarily going to help you understand a particular individual at a particular time. There will be occasions when a person will leave you baffled, disappointed or astonished. When this happens, it is natural to cast around for an explanation for

the person's behaviour – any explanation. Our desire to understand each other springs, in the first place, from our need as social animals to predict what others will do next, and it is just too uncomfortable to remain in a state of unknowing. As a result, we reach for whatever psychiatric diagnoses are currently popular – 'anxious', 'bipolar' – and apply them to people we disapprove of or don't understand. Once we have done that, we make sure that we only see those parts of the person that confirm our belief about them.

This is not people-reading; it is labelling. Far from helping you understand the person, giving them a label often obscures what's really going on in the person's mind.

This, then, is a cautionary word about reading too much into an individual's behaviour – especially the odd, one-off event. Remember that the behaviour a person displays during a business meeting may be quite different to their behaviour at a party, and until you have seen someone

Our desire to understand each other springs, in the first place, from our need as social animals to predict what others will do next, and it is just too uncomfortable to remain in a state of unknowing.

in many different circumstances and noted patterns of behaviour you cannot know them. So when you meet someone new, try to remain for a while in the uncomfortable zone of uncertainty.

Remember too, that there is a very simple way of finding out about someone: ask. A lot of people suffer from 'transparency illusion' – the notion that their thoughts, feelings and intentions are crystal clear to others just because they know them (or think they do). They might be quite surprised to discover that other people have gathered quite wrong ideas about them, and be very pleased to explain themselves if you offer them the chance.

Remember too, that what applies to other also applies to you. So if you want to read people at an individual level, ensure that you are 'writing' yourself clearly for them to read too.

BIBLIOGRAPHY

Ambady, Nalini, and Skowronski, John J. (eds) *First Impressions* (Guilford Press, 2008)

Ariely, Dan *Predictably Irrational: The Hidden Forces That Shape Our Decisions* (Harper, 2009)

Baron-Cohen, Simon *The Essential Difference: Men, Women and the Extreme Male Brain* (Penguin, 2012)

Byron, Christopher M. *Testosterone Inc: Tales of CEOs Gone Wild* (Wiley, 2008)

Carré, Justin M., and McCormick, Cheryl M. *'In your face: facial metrics predict aggressive behaviour in the laboratory and in varsity and professional hockey players.'* Proceedings of the Royal Society B 2008; 2785(1651).

Choleris, Elena, Pfaff, Donald W., and Kavaliers, Martin Oxytocin, *Vasopressin and Related Peptides in the Regulation of Behavior* (Cambridge University Press, 2013)

Cialdini, Robert *Pre-Suasion: A Revolutionary Way to Influence and Persuade* (Random House Business, 2016)

Clearfield, Dylan *Micro-expressions: Reading Anyone's Secret Thoughts* (G. Stempien Publishing Company, 2015)

Costa, Paul T., and Widiger, Thomas A. (eds) *Personality Disorders and the Five-Factor Model of Personality* (American Psychological Association, 2012)

Dael, N., Mortillaro, M., and Scherer, K.R. *'Emotion expression in body action and posture.'* Emotion 2012; 12(5):1085–1101.

Daniels, David, and Price, Virginia *The Essential Enneagram: The Definitive Personality Test and Self-Discovery Guide* (HarperOne, 2009)

Draper, Michael *How to Analyze People: Analyze & Read People with Human Psychology, Body Language, and the 6 Human Needs* (CreateSpace Independent Publishing Platform, 2015)

De Raad, Boele, and Perugini, *Marco Big Five Assessment* (Hogrefe & Huber, 2002)

Doherty, Martin J. *Theory of Mind: How Children Understand Others' Thoughts and Feelings* (Psychology Press, 2008)

Ekman, P., Friesen, W.V., O'Sullivan, M., et al. *'Universals and cultural differences in the judgments of facial expressions of emotion.'* Journal of Personality and Social Psychology 1987; 53(4):712–17

Fischhoff, B., Slovic, P., and Lichtenstein, S. *'Knowing with certainty: The appropriateness of extreme confidence.'* Journal of Experimental Psychology: Human Perception and Performance 1977; 3(4):552–64

Garhart Mooney, Carol *Theories of Attachment: An Introduction to to Bowlby, Ainsworth, Gerber, Brazelton, Kennell, and Klaus* (Redleaf Press, 2009)

Gillibrand, Rachel *Developmental Psychology* (Pearson, 2016)

Gilovich, Thomas. *How We Know What Isn't So: Fallibility of Human Reason in Everyday Life* (Free Press, 1993)

Gilovich, Thomas, and Ross, Lee *The Wisest One in the Room: How To Harness Psychology's Most Powerful Insights* (Oneworld Publications, 2016)

Hadnagy, Christopher *Social Engineering: The Art of Human Hacking* (John Wiley & Sons, 2010)

Hallinan, Joseph T. *Why We Make Mistakes: How We Look Without Seeing, Forget Things in Seconds, and Are All Pretty Sure We Are Way Above Average* (Broadway Books, 2010)

Hassin, R., and Trope, Y. *'Facing faces: Studies on the cognitive aspects of physiognomy.'* Journal of Personality and Social Psychology 2000; 78 (5):837–52

Hinshelwood, R.D., Robinson, Susan, and Zarate, Oscar. *Introducing Melanie Klein: A Graphic Guide* (Icon Books Ltd, 2011)

Howard, Pierce J., and Mitchell Howard, Jane *The Owner's Manual for Personality at Work: How the Big Five Personality Traits Affect Performance, Communication, Teamwork, Leadership, and Sales* (Bard Press, 2000)

Hurlemann, Rene, and Grinevich, Valery *Behavioral Pharmacology of Neuropeptides: Oxytocin (Current Topics in Behavioral Neurosciences)* (Springer, 2017)

Keating, C.F. *'Gender and the Physiognomy of Dominance and Attractiveness.'* Social Psychology Quarterly 1985; 48(1):61–70

Kroeger, Otto, and Thuesen, Janet M. *Type Talk: The*

16 Personality Types That Determine How We Live, Love, and Work (Dell, 2013)

Lapworth, Phil, and Sills, Charlotte *An Introduction to Transactional Analysis: Helping People Change* (Sage Publications Ltd, 2011)

Lefevre, C.E., Lewis, G.J., Perrett, D.I., et al *'Telling facial metrics: facial width is associated with testosterone levels in men.'* Evolution and Human Behavior 2013; 34(4):273–79.

Loeb, Daniel E *Deception Detection: A Pocket Guide to Statement Analysis, Micro-expressions, Body Language, Interviews and Interrogations.* (CreateSpace Independent Publishing Platform, 2013)

Lowe, Gordon R. *'Eye colour and personality.'* Personality and Individual Differences 2010; 49(1): 59–64.

Martin, Everett Dean *The Behavior of Crowds; A Psychological Study* (Martino Fine Books, 2014)

McGarty, Craig (ed) *Stereotypes as Explanations: The Formation of Meaningful Beliefs about Social Groups* (Cambridge University Press, 2002)

Mcraney, David *You Are Not So Smart: Why Your Memory Is Mostly Fiction, Why You Have Too Many Friends On Facebook And 46 Other Ways You're Deluding Yourself* (Oneworld Publications, 2012)

Nahai, Nathalie *Webs of Influence: The Psychology of Online Persuasion* (Pearson Business, 2017)

Penton-Voak, L.S., Jones, B.C., Little, A.C., et al. *'Symmetry, sexual dimorphism in facial proportions and male facial attractiveness.'* Evolution and Human Behavior 1999; 20(5):295–307.

Pitterman, Hallee, and Nowicki Jr, Stephen. *'A Test of the Ability to Identify Emotion in Human Standing and Sitting Postures: The Diagnostic Analysis of Nonverbal Accuracy-2 Posture Test (DANVA2-POS).'* Genetic, Social, and General Psychology Monographs 2004;130(2):146–62.

Rauthmann, J.R., Seubert, C.T., Sachse, P., et al. *'Eyes as windows to the soul: Gazing behavior is related to personality.'* Journal of Research in Personality 2012; 46(2): 147–156.

Reason, James *Human Error* (Cambridge University Press, 1991)

Runciman, W.G., Maynard Smith, J., and Dunbar, R.I.M. *Evolution of Social Behaviour Patterns in Primates and Man* (British Academy, 1996)

Schulz, Kathryn *Being Wrong: Adventures in the Margin of Error: The Meaning of Error in an Age of Certainty* (Portobello Books Ltd, 2011)

Schyns, B., and Sanders, K. *'In the Eyes of the Beholder: Personality and the Perception of Leadership.'* Journal of Applied Social Psychology 2007; 37(10):2345–63.

Stangor, Charles (ed) *Stereotypes and Prejudice: Essential Readings* (Routledge, 2000)

Stewart, Ian, and Joines, Vann T A *Today: A New Introduction to Transactional Analysis* (Lifespace Publishing, 2012)

Sunstein, Cass R., and Hastie, Reid *Wiser: Getting Beyond Groupthink to Make Groups Smarter* (Harvard Business Review Press, 2014)

Tsvetkov, Yanko *Atlas of Prejudice: The Complete Stereotype Map Collection* (Alphadesigner, 2017)

Uvnäs-Moberg, Kerstin *Oxytocin: The Biological Guide To Motherhood* (Praeclarus Press, 2016)

Vedantam, Shankar *The Hidden Brain: How Our Unconscious Minds Elect Presidents, Control Markets, Wage Wars, and Save Our Lives* (Spiegel & Grau, 2010)

Weinschenk, Susan *How to Get People to Do Stuff: Master the art and science of persuasion and motivation* (New Riders, 2013)

Wezowski, Kasia, and Wezowski, Patryk *The Micro Expressions Book for Business* (New Vision, 2012)

Widiger, Thomas A. (ed) *The Oxford Handbook of the Five Factor Model* (Oxford University Press, 2017)

Wiggins, Jerry S *The Five-Factor Model Of Personality: The Theoretical Perspectives* (Guildford Press, 1996)

Willis, J., and Toderov, A. *'Making Up Your Mind After a 100-Ms Exposure to a Face.'* Psychological Science 2006; 17(7):592–98.

Winnicott, D.W. *The Family and Individual Development* (Routledge, 2006)

At BUILD+BECOME we believe in building knowledge that helps you navigate your world.

Our books help you make sense of the changing world around you by taking you from concept to real-life application through 20 accessible lessons designed to make you think. Create your library of knowledge.

BUILD + BECOME

www.buildbecome.com
buildbecome@quarto.com

@buildbecome
@QuartoExplores

Using a unique, visual approach, Gerald Lynch explains the most important tech developments of the modern world – examining their impact on society and how, ultimately, we can use technology to achieve our full potential.

From the driverless transport systems hitting our roads to the nanobots and artificial intelligence pushing human capabilities to their limits, in 20 dip-in lessons this book introduces the most exciting and important technological concepts of our age, helping you to better understand the world around you today, tomorrow and in the decades to come.

Gerald Lynch is a technology and science journalist, and is currently Senior Editor of technology website TechRadar. Previously Editor of websites Gizmodo UK and Tech Digest, he has also written for publications such as *Kotaku* and *Lifehacker*, and is a regular technology pundit for the BBC. Gerald was on the judging panel for the James Dyson Award. He lives with his wife in London.

GERALD LYNCH

BUILD +
BECOME

GET TECHNOLOGY

BE IN THE KNOW.
UPGRADE YOUR FUTURE.

KNOW TECHNOLOGY TODAY, TO EQUIP YOURSELF FOR TOMORROW.

Using a unique, visual approach to explore philosophical concepts, Adam Ferner shows how philosophy is one of our best tools for responding to the challenges of the modern world.

From philosophical 'people skills' to ethical and moral questions about our lifestyle choices, philosophy teaches us to ask the right questions, even if it doesn't necessarily hold all the answers. With 20 dip-in lessons from history's great philosophers alongside today's most pioneering thinkers, this book will guide you to think deeply and differently.

Adam Ferner has worked in academic philosophy both in France and the UK – but it's philosophy *outside* the academy that he enjoys the most. In addition to his scholarly research, he writes regularly for *The Philosophers' Magazine* and teaches in schools and youth centres in London.

ADAM FERNER

BUILD + BECOME

THINK DIFFERENTLY

OPEN YOUR MIND. PHILOSOPHY FOR MODERN LIFE.

PHILOSOPHY IS ABOUT OUR LIVES AND HOW WE LIVE THEM.

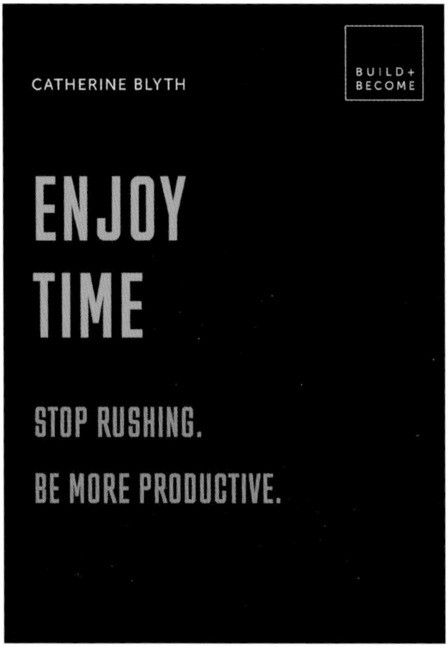

CATHERINE BLYTH
BUILD+ BECOME
ENJOY TIME
STOP RUSHING.
BE MORE PRODUCTIVE.

October 2018

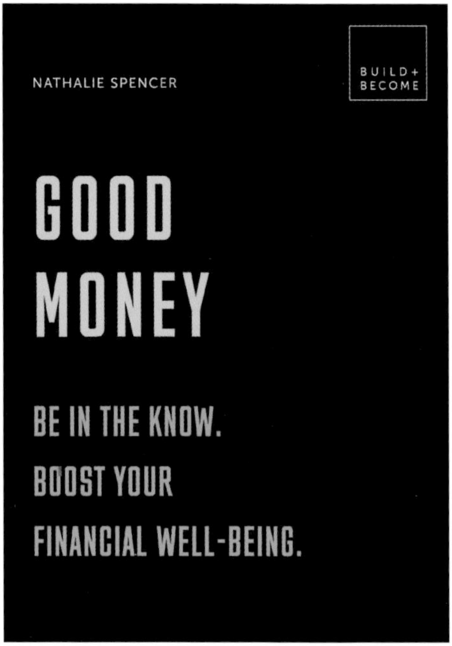

NATHALIE SPENCER
BUILD+ BECOME
GOOD MONEY
BE IN THE KNOW.
BOOST YOUR FINANCIAL WELL-BEING.

October 2018

Through a series of 20 practical and effective exercises, all using a unique visual approach, Michael Atavar challenges you to open your mind, shift your perspective and ignite your creativity. Whatever your passion, craft or aims, this book will expertly guide you from bright idea, through the tricky stages of development, to making your concepts a reality.

We often treat creativity as if it was something separate from us – in fact it is, as this book demonstrates, incredibly simple: creativity is nothing other than the very core of 'you'.

Michael Atavar is an artist and author. He has written four books on creativity – *How to Be an Artist, 12 Rules of Creativity, Everyone Is Creative* and *How to Have Creative Ideas in 24 Steps – Better Magic.* He also designed (with Miles Hanson) a set of creative cards *'210CARDS'*.

He works 1-2-1, runs workshops and gives talks about the impact of creativity on individuals and organisations. www.creativepractice.com

MICHAEL ATAVAR

BUILD +
BECOME

BEING CREATIVE

BE INSPIRED.
UNLOCK YOUR
ORIGINALITY.

CREATIVITY BEGINS WITH YOU.

08
BUILD +
BECOME

CRUMBS, IDEAS

There is no part of creativity that is not about looking, paying attention, noticing. So pull into your world view the everyday – the materials that surround you, what arrives on the pavement, the pieces of the world.

Do this first by recording, writing in your notepad.

+ THE EXERCISE

One trick I have for achieving this I call 'assisted seeing', and it goes like this:

Spend one minute recording what you see.

Write continuously.

Keep your eyes glued to what you are recording, ignoring everything else. I find this helps. It doesn't matter if the words are illegible on the page. Simply make the paper an action event, directed by your writing.

The task is not to stop, allowing all mistakes that arrive – these errors can then be folded back into your practice in a coherent way.

This 'assisted seeing' can be extended for 1, 2, 3, 5, 10 minutes, if you can tolerate it.

(If you could imagine doing this every day, you are on your way to making a longer commitment to writing.)

You might think that faced with the blankness of your own experience you would find nothing. Yet, that's not what I have discovered. When you look with your own eyes, you see something in an original way.

Time slows down, the moment grows, everything expands.

I often attempt this exercise when I find myself alone in a café, waiting for someone to arrive. In the few garbled minutes, I record what's happening. It's a form of concentrated looking and has resulted in some of my most personal, intense, solo experiences.

When you limit yourself to only one area of practice, say 'action', you will be creative only until this reservoir of activity dries up; then you will have no internal process to work with.

Although this sounds an unlikely scenario (how can action ever be wrong?), it's a common problem in business environments.

If you hit a brick wall, and things don't work as before, it's because the barrier represents a challenge to feeling. When you deal with what's inside, the problem usually evaporates.

I remember recently sitting in a West End fast-food chain with big windows overlooking the street, observing the church opposite and writing in my notepad, simply noting my own impressions.

(Sometimes I don't bother to look at the paper.)

I recalled the name of the building opposite, 'Church of the Assumption' – and so following my own process, I reflected on the following question: what had I previously assumed to be correct? This is a good example of process in action – I wrote a list of these 'assumed' things, 20 items running down the page in one long ladder.

In this stillness, the flash of the moment, I was inside my own creativity, absorbed in the narrowness of now.

It also shows how several of the actions that you have learnt so far in the book can be combined into one complex activity:

> Lists
> Assisted seeing
> Process
> Internal camera
> Action

When you activate the creative, you are not staying in one domain – you are mutating forms, melting, jumping between experiences, using several skills. It's this crucible, activated physically, that begets creativity.

08
BUILD +
BECOME

CURIOUS, OPEN, UNDECIDED

If you feel that you don't have the skills to attempt these tasks, a short cut to process is to work with colour.

Colour runs riot through boundaries, pushing you forward in direct, unconditional ways.

+ THE EXERCISE

Quickly pick three colours from your immediate environment:

> **High-res orange**
> **Dirty white**
> **Painted wood edge**
> **Yellow dot**
> **Intense, hard red**

(It doesn't matter what you choose.)

Make a narrative cluster from the three colours: not necessarily a story, more an impression, a sense of connectivity – a common feeling that they might all contain. Finally, pick one colour from the selection, look at it directly, let it hold your entire field of vision, close up to your eyes, and absorb it.

Then go back several sections to page 44, and combine your three words from that exercise with the final colour selected here.

Put the words and the colour physically on the table.

Perhaps it's the colour choice 'High-res orange' with the words:

> **'Curious'**?
> **'Open'**?
> **'Undecided'**?

What do the colour and the words mean to you?

Is there any journey that you have made while reading Part Two of this book that is reflected here in the choices in front of you?

If so, what?

60

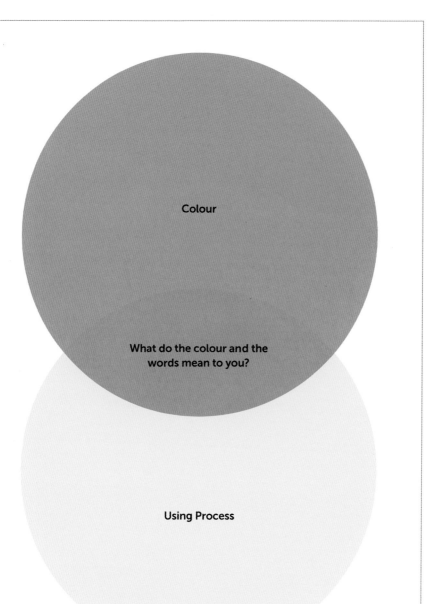

Colour

What do the colour and the
words mean to you?

Using Process

61

ACKNOWLEDGEMENTS

My thanks to all those brilliant researchers whose work I have drawn on for this book, to Peter Tallack of the Science Factory, to my Editor Lucy Warburton for her painstaking care and attention to detail, and to Richard for (he claims) taking on board various tedious tasks to give me space to work on this.

Rita Carter is an award-winning medical and science writer, lecturer and broadcaster who specialises in the human brain: what it does, how it does it, and why. She is the author of *Mind Mapping* and has hosted a series of science lectures for public audience. Rita lives in the UK.